Simple, practical ways to enhance family life

Celebrating Families

Helen Sanderson and Maye Taylor

First published in Great Britain in 2008 by HSA Press

ISBN 978-1-906514-03-7

Text © Helen Sanderson and Maye Taylor

Photographs © Anne Bennison Photography and HSA Foundation

Life Map images on page 119 reprinted with kind permission from Continuum Books.

PATH format illustration on page 127 is taken from *Person Centred Planning with MAPS and PATH, A Workbook for Facilitators* published by Inclusion Press and is used with permission from the authors; John O'Brien and Jack Pearpoint.

Some of this information has been taken from Essential Lifestyle Planning for Everyone, Smull and Sanderson, 2005. The materials on person centred thinking and essential lifestyle planning were developed by The Learning Community for Person Centred Practices and are used with permission. www.learningcommunity.us

Printed in Scotland by Scotprint

HSA Press

34 Broomfield Road

Heaton Moor

Stockport

Cheshire

SK4 4ND

www.celebratingfamilies.co.uk

Contents

Where we're coming from

Helen

Of all my roles – wife, mother, employer, colleague, friend – being a Mum is the most challenging, significant and rewarding one. In my work, I use approaches called `person centred thinking and planning´. These tools have been invaluable for me as a parent, as well as at work, and I wanted to share them. So my vision for Celebrating Families was to create something practical and useful for parents and their families. I wanted this to be a book that would share credible approaches, and ways of recording them, that parents could use with ease.

Maye

As a parent you have a definite place: in the wrong. Not only will your children tell you that, but experts will come along and reinforce it, telling you that what you have been doing is wrong, and that you need to do it all differently. In the hope that you will find strategies that you too can use, this book takes the risk of revealing what we have been doing, that we think works. It is published in just that spirit: this worked for us. Neither of us pretends to speak for all parents. Clearly the stories in this book are located in the economic and social conditions, times and places of the people who tell them.

Helen and Maye

These stories collect the experiences of many and, as it is the stories and ideas, rather than who tells them, that matter, the voices are all mixed together. These are loud voices telling family stories, and relating attempts to negotiate the path between nurturing our children as unique individuals and socialising them to survive in a world that can be harsh and hostile. The book celebrates the people telling the stories, the individuals in them and the ideas and suggestions that emerge. It is designed to help you be the parent you want to be.

We hope you will find Celebrating Families easy to use and fun to read. Every tool in it involves practical and creative ideas for helping children and developing family life; the stories, activities and exercises you will find here are shared in order to make that as straightforward as possible. Our hope is that, through you using these strategies in the right spirit, they may help your family do things differently, and trust that in this case `differently´ will also mean better.

Chapter 1

Stop The World
We Want To Get Off

This is a personal book, which aims to share ideas, concerns, stories, and visions. Let's start with our concerns about the impact of living in a consumer society obsessed with celebrity - a concern you will find running throughout the book.

The need for meaning in life was once met through social ties and networks, but it seems to us that these aspects of community are being progressively swamped by cultural systems such as the media and advertising. We need what we can buy. By buying the product we buy into the culture and thus construct our identities. This need is not just for the material goods in themselves but for the meaning and status that having them bestows. The designer label has become the symbol of success. It says, 'Look I can afford this.' There is even a designer label toilet brush that costs £200 - and people buy it. In our consumer society status and worth are achieved by what you can afford, what you have, not what you are and do. This is the message that all the parents in this book are struggling against. The advertising industry, which persuades us that we need what we don't, is very comfortable with spending millions of pounds targeting children. Remonstrate with marketers about the emergence of 'pester power' and you are met with, 'Well it's up to parents to say no.'

The other part of the equation we are dealing with here is the cult of celebrity, and there is no doubt that celebrity sells. Advertising is not a social service; it is a market activity. If it makes money, it works. As an example of the fact that celebrity sells, take David Beckham, a celebrity who, just by being famous, is held up in the media as a role model on a whole range of topics, from pregnancy and childcare through sports and fashion on into government and politics. Here, a person whose fame has come from excelling in one area is suddenly regarded as an expert on a whole range of other things. Celebrity is now so central to our culture that many seek to become famous for its own sake. In media circuses like Big Brother, wannabes who can survive being thrown into the lions' den of the Big Brother house may emerge to have well-paid careers as celebrities - even though they haven't actually excelled at anything. In the twenty-first century, as Andy Warhol prophesied, everyone may be famous for fifteen minutes - but famous, often, only for being famous.

At the same time, it is difficult to read a newspaper, listen to the radio or watch television without coming across urgent voices expressing concern over what is happening to the traditional family in contemporary society. Discussion of the family seems to be characterised by fear and fascination, but the persistent appeal of something called 'family' remains, and the term now applies to quite diverse domestic arrangements. This would seem to suggest that as a society we cannot imagine ordering our lives outside the norm of some kind of family. The media bemoan the demise of the alleged golden age: the idealised 1950s family, where marriages were for life, the man was head of the household, and as such responsible for his wife and children. His role was to be in the labour market, while the woman's was to stay at home looking after the housework and children - and everything was wonderful. A tremendous yearning is often expressed for the order and certainty that this golden age seems to represent. The concept of family appears to be passing the fit-for-purpose test. In that traditional model of family, where the men were the sole breadwinners, the relationship between fathers and children could be difficult. The social context of the past two or three decades has altered the gender stereotypes of men and women, changing roles and revealing capacities previously hidden behind a strict, stereotypical understanding of parenting. Although nurture now seems to be becoming more equitably distributed between mothers and fathers, the emphasis is still on the mother as primary care-giver. (And how that role has changed.) Reflecting the primacy of mothers as nurturers, this book is largely composed of mothers' voices. So let's hear a few of them discussing being a mother in our contemporary, celebrity-obsessed consumer society.

Sheena tells it like it is: 'Unlike Victoria Beckham, when my baby was five months old I did not weigh less than I had before I was pregnant and the only thing that fitted me were my husband's tracksuit bottoms. My sweatshirt was covered in baby-sick and there, staring at me from the racks of women's magazines, were pictures showing perfectly groomed actresses with their miracle babies, declaring that motherhood was sexy.'

Jo can remember falling into a pit of despair about the gap between the highly romanticised and absurd ideals of perfect motherhood and the reality of her every-day life: 'The message I was battered with was that however much we do for and love our kids, it's never enough.' The unattainable ideal of mother love is one of infinite patience and adoration and it doesn't stop there. To be a remotely decent mother, you need to acquire the skills of the therapist, paediatrician, consumer product safety inspector, and child development specialist. Marketing requires you to search out everything from orthodontically correct teething rings to Maths flash cards for six months old infants. Perfect mothers build perfect children and buy better toys. But buy too many and the children are spoilt; too few, or the wrong ones, and the children will be developmentally challenged. Not in the pages of this book.

The explosion of celebrity motherhood promotes the idyll of eternally joyful, stress-free motherhood. Maye says that fortunately when she was a mother of young children in the 1970s, there were few celebrity mothers on the covers of magazines. Nowadays, they are everywhere, declaring to camera that they love being mothers much more than their work, fame or fortune, and that they would spend every single second with their child if they didn't have the nuisance of that movie to finish.

If we aren't constantly ecstatic about motherhood, if we have a teaspoonful of ambivalence about it, it's thought that there's something really wrong. And now you can't even be a fat Grandma - Jane Fonda has a lot to answer for. Whatever happened to gaining wisdom with the years? Why is being sexy more important than that? Presumably, while expensive cosmetic treatments are commercially exploitable, acquiring wisdom is not.

As we suggested above, families do not exist in a vacuum. We have written this book in a climate of mother-blaming; motherhood is revered, but - sadly - mothers are still denigrated. There is help for the struggling mother, in the form of classes and how-to books on parenting, not to mention television's Supernanny, and then, if all else fails, there are fines for those who get it wrong.

Our concept of celebrating does not turn a blind eye to reality - neither of us is naïve enough to ignore the horror stories - nor is it couched in the language of Mary Poppins. But, by telling some stories and highlighting some techniques that have helped us and our colleagues and friends, it is an attempt to encapsulate the enormous responsibility involved in being a parent. And we hope we have done it in a way that celebrates the lives of the people involved. We want to share what we do well, what we know works and what we know just doesn't. Nothing we say here is in the tone of the expert. The 'we' of these pages have laughed and cried together. Sometimes we've just chuckled over those pictures of celebrity mothers; of course we all love our children, but we don't have to shape carrots into fir trees to put into their packed lunches to prove it.

So here we want to tell true stories of family life. Yes, being a Mum is good; but it's exhausting, exasperating, wildly under-appreciated and usually anything but sexy. The chapters that follow are about what parenting has involved for us, and the families in these stories.

Chapter 2

Sharing What We Know

In 1995 Helen Harcombe, a terminally ill mother, wrote a 'Mummy Manual' for the husband she would leave behind. She gave him instructions on how to look after their seven-year-old daughter, Ffion. Helen wrote about school uniforms, bathing and how to do Ffion's hair, stuff that most fathers would not notice. For example, she told her husband: 'Be sure to chuck out Ffion's old school uniforms - no daughter of mine to look scruffy - bath and hair wash every other night - no child of mine to be smelly.' She added strict guidelines on how to put up Ffion's hair: 'Neat parting, no bump, use tail comb if necessary...and no straggly bits.'

Helen had written the job description for her own life, and many mothers - ourselves included - cried when they read it. This book is about what families can do well, and in celebrating families, Helen's 'Mummy Manual' identifies and acknowledges the mother as the repository of expert knowledge within the family. Which might be a good place to start. What are mothers expert in?

Maye asked a group of mothers to brainstorm what they do. She emphasised that she wanted them to think not of the qualities they brought to the role, nor indeed their level of competence, just to think out loud about what they actually had to do. Here's what they came up with:

challenging
washing
teaching
loving
budgeting
soothing
egg shell walking
watching
sympathising
mending
motivating
mind reading
playing
advocating
anticipating
resolving conflicts
remembering everything
keep up to date
infuriating
learning
withholding
diagnose
cooking
juggling
record keeping
nurse
controlling
take flak
disappointing
rewarding
cleaning
encouraging
wiping
understanding
get things wrong
win the mothers race at sports day
shopping
punishing
get things right
protecting
inspecting
pleasing
make judgments

What would you add to this list? And if this were a job specification, would you apply for the job?

As Helen Harcombe was dying, in order that her child might have consistency of care, she wrote a detailed description of her own role. This need for consistency of care is paramount; even if they cannot agree on anything else, all experts agree on this. Helen's specification was extraordinary in the circumstances, but in many ways every mother who shares the upbringing of her children with others does the same. You have to tell the grandparents, nursery, child-minder, nanny, school – and sometimes even the father.

Yet few of us write these instructions down. So it is easy for them to be forgotten or misinterpreted. It's certain though that if we don't record how we want our child cared for, it will be unlikely to happen. What is not said cannot be heard. (All right, saying it is no guarantee that it will be acted on - but it is a start.) Your child may be in the hands of skilled nursery nurses, loving grandparents or qualified teachers, but you are still the expert, and you have information that can enable everyone who looks after them to do so better. Just the process of examining what we know matters can help clarify priorities and thus get closer to that all-important balance in life.

Josh

Sarah and Adam were worried about Josh. Since his birth they had constantly been at the GP's surgery – and in and out of hospital with everything from common baby ailments to significant illnesses. He was beautiful and adorable. He cried a lot, too, so Sarah was exhausted and tearful. She was coming to the end of her maternity leave and the date with the red circle that said 'Back to work' loomed ever closer. She had already found a nursery for Josh, but how would they be able to cope? Josh cried so much.

In desperation, Sarah phoned an old colleague, Ruth, who came round with a bottle of wine and pizza. Ruth, Sarah and Adam sat around the kitchen table for two hours, talking about Josh. Ruth had her laptop and typed as they talked. The conversation led to questions and decisions on how they could use this document to help settle Josh into nursery. The three of them recorded in detail what anyone who was looking after Josh would need to know – all about his routines and how to look after him. Ruth is a bit of a whiz on the computer, and also created a 'Josh' poster.

To begin with, Sarah thought that what they had produced would be very useful for nursery, but she quickly saw how much it would also help Granny, who baby-sat for them every week. The information described the balance between what matters to Josh, and the help he needs to be well.

WHAT IS IMPORTANT TO JOSH

- Playing in water and seeing the lights in the pool at Water Babies every week.
- Having a play in the bath every night.
- Having Loopy Lou and Mr Lion with him in his cot at night, and sometimes in his car seat.
- Chewing anything - particularly Sophie the giraffe. Sophie goes with Josh everywhere except nursery.
- Bright lights - flashing.
- Bold colours - particularly red.
- Music and being sung to - the Grand Old Duke of York, and the Wheels on the Bus, and Mum singing "Who's that boy?" and "You are my Joshy".
- Being outside everyday, regardless of the weather - being in a sling and seeing the leaves and hearing the wind.
- Watching things move - fans with blowy things, wind up train set.
- Being snuggled and kissed on the cheek.
- Having raspberries blown on his chest or neck.
- Playing peekaboo.
- Batting toys under his play gym.
- Yoghurt and sweet things.

JOSH

WHAT WE LOVE ABOUT JOSH

- Tries really hard - very determined
- Fantastic laugh - makes you melt
- Cheeky smile
- Resilient
- Energetic
- Cuddly and snuggly
- Strong - vice-like grip!
- Does not give up
- Gorgeous face with beautiful eyes
- Great to swim with
- Bright
- Observant

WHAT YOU NEED TO KNOW OR DO TO LOOK AFTER JOSH

ABOUT SLEEP

- He needs a sleep during the day every 2 to 2.5 hours, even if this is just for 10 minutes (usually this is for about 20 - 30 minutes).
- Catch him before he gets over tired. When he is tired he will rub his eyes and yawn, and then start to moan and thrash his arms and legs. When he gets really over tired he will start to thrash more vigorously and throw himself backwards. At the first sign try and help him go to sleep. You can lie him down in a cot with a blanket, play music, 'shhh' him and stroke his head. Occasionally use a dummy. He falls asleep in the car for 45 minutes or an hour if you are moving. He can fall asleep in the buggy as well. Sometimes taking him outside for a few moments will calm and cool him down and help settle him.

IF JOSH WAKES UP

- If Josh wakes up and cries, leave him for a couple of minutes, to see if he goes back off to sleep. If his crying tone changes and becomes more intense, go to him.
- Try to settle him without getting him out of bed, stroke his head, give him Loopy Lou or his dummy. If you cannot settle him in bed, get him out and put him over your shoulder and see if you can pat him to sleep. If this does not work, he could be hungry, give him a bottle.

NIGHT-TIME ROUTINE

Before he goes in the bath get the medicines, milk and towels ready. He has a bath around 7pm. He has floating toys in the bath and a bath chair. We do the 'water babies' routine (say "Joshua...ready...go pause and then pour a little water over his face. Do this three times). After his bath he gets wrapped in his snuggly towel, onto the change mat with his mobile, read him a story (current favourite is Baby Bright). Massage his legs with baby oil. Put him in his sleeping bag. Offer him some milk (he may or may not have this). Give him his medicine Ranitidine 0.4 mls and Trimethoprim 1.2 mls) in a syringe. Space these out so they are not together.

"JOSH'S LAUGH MAKES YOU MELT"

QUESTIONS TO ANSWER

1. Does Josh want Loopy Lou or Sophie with him at nursery (or another toy).
2. Would singing the Grand Old Duke of York, or playing a recording of us singing it, help him go back to sleep when he wakes.
3. Could we play CDs to him more during breakfast?
4. How can we help Josh settle into nursery better?
5. Should we cut down/stop the ranitidine?

EATING AND DRINKING

- Josh has gastric reflux and this means that sometimes he is sick after eating. Sometimes he eats and is sick straight away; sometimes he is sick up to a couple of hours later.
- Eating little and often and keeping him upright for a while after meals helps.
- He has 4 little meals a day at approx 8.30, 12noon, 3pm and 5.30pm.
- Yoghurts and creamy sauces especially make him sick (Soya yoghurt is not as bad).
- He has a sweet tooth and we are trying to build his weight up.
- He has his milk in between his meals - usually 100 oz of Nutramigin (number 2) but he does not always want this.
- As Josh also has kidney reflux he must have 500mls of fluid a day so if he does not want milk try very weak blackcurrant juice instead.

ACTION

1
TO EXPLORE JOSH GOING TO NURSERY ALMOST FULL TIME FOR 2 WEEKS WITH PARENTS TO HELP TO SETTLE HIM IN BEFORE CHRISTMAS

2
TO ASK JOSH'S AUNT FOR INFORMATION ON WHERE WE CAN GET ANOTHER SOPHIE

Sarah said: 'It is the best two hours I have ever spent. The poster looked fantastic and really captured who Josh was. It is now on his nursery wall and has been a great way to introduce new babysitters to him. My brother babysat last week for the first time and I used the poster to explain how to settle Josh into his cot when he wakes at night. But one of the nicest and most unexpected aspects of what we've done is looking back at our first poster and seeing how much he has changed in six months.'

Andrew was pleased, too: 'I cannot believe how quickly we captured who Josh was and come up with solutions to problems we had been struggling with. It really was a two hour chat that resulted in us being able to say what mattered to Josh and from there we worked out a plan and a way forward.'

Nursery staff said: 'The poster was a great way to find out about Josh when he first came to us. We have kept a copy at nursery as it helps new staff know what to do when they first meet him.'

Details, Details, Details

It's the detail that makes the difference. Instructions on how to look after your child are only effective when they contain so much detail that nothing is left to chance. Instead of just 'Put Ffion's hair up in the morning', Helen recorded the specific detail: 'Neat parting, no bump, use tail comb if necessary…and no straggly bits.' It mattered to Ffion's Mum that there were no straggly bits.

The guide to caring for Josh, that his parents produced for the nursery, gives detail on how to soothe him to sleep: 'Stroke his brow and give him Loopy Lou.' If you want to write your own, there are some ideas on the following page.

Shannon

Lori was moving to Birmingham. This meant taking her daughter, Shannon, out of nursery and away from her friends. For lots of reasons the move was great, but Lori was losing sleep over how Shannon would adjust. Her new job meant that she would have to get a nanny or a childminder, and she was worried about how she would afford that. She decided that she needed to do something positive instead of just worrying.

One Friday night Lori watched Charlotte Church on television. Charlotte sat in a room watching a woman in a restaurant. Charlotte could see and hear everything that was happening and, as part of an elaborate joke, was giving instructions to the woman through an earpiece.

Write enough detail so that if, in an emergency, your neighbour suddenly had to look after your child and you had no time to tell them anything, they would have all the information they needed to stand in for you.

If you want, put in pictures or photographs.

Describe the what, where, who, when and how of caring for your child.

Be specific: rather than 'favourite toy' say which one it is; instead of 'friends', list them.

Use bullet points with detail, but don't write War and Peace. If you get up to 20 pages, it's too long!

Cluster things under headings to make it easier for people to follow, but don't try to group everything; life isn't so neat and there will be things that stand alone.

'That's it,' thought Lori. 'I'll write everything down, as if I had an earpiece to a nanny, and could advise and instruct her on how to look after Shannon throughout the day.' Here's what Lori wrote:

Looking After Shannon

- Shannon prefers to eat little & often (as opposed to a bigger meal at meatimes). Some of her favourites are: sausages, eggs, carrots, pasta and custard. It's best not to force her to eat, or make an issue of it.
- Shannon has a nap at around 12.30 pm for about an hour and a half and goes to bed at 8pm.
- She has a bath every night and, although she doesn't really like making her way there, she often enjoys it once she's in the bath. Tell her "it's bath time" and then allow her some independence: she prefers to get undressed and into the bath herself. However, you will need to stand beside her to make sure she doesn't slip. Once in the bath Shannon likes playing with tubs and empty plastic bottles.
- When she gets upset, it is usually because she is tired or frustrated when struggling to do things herself. Bend down and give her eye contact, talk in a quiet voice and try to figure out what's wrong. When upset, Shannon doesn't like a fuss, so keep conversation to a minimum initially. If she needs help remind her to ask for it next time. Often when upset, she needs you to offer her a way out of the situation. So, after 2 or 3 minutes, ask her if she wants a cuddle.
- Sometimes you need to remind Shannon not to shout. Again what works is to get down to her level and gain eye contact. Then, talking to her in a calm, quiet voice, ask her not to shout and respond to what she wants when she stops shouting.

Lori sifted her information about how to support Shannon in order to imagine what the perfect nanny or person would be like. (Although she also wanted the child-minder to know: who Shannon was; what was important to her; and how to look after her.) She thought about the characteristics, the skills and the interests that the perfect child-minder would need. She knew she would never find this perfect person, but she thought the following checklist would be a good place to start.

Looking After Shannon

From this information Lori devised a list of questions to ask potential child-minders so that she could best match them to what Shannon needed and what she needed as a Mum.

common interests

1. loves being around other children
2. being in the garden - even in the cold
3. music, singing and having a boogie
4. curling up and watching DVDs.

skills you need to have

• Flexible - in your approach and with hours you can work (especially mornings and tea time).

• reliable and punctual very important to us as a family.

• a good cook (someone who won't outshine me!) and will give Shanni a balanced varied diet with food she likes ♡.

• good at making learning fun...

• can plan ahead and will get things done - working around Shannis routines.

• preferably able to drive. -

Characteristics you need to have

- preferably female
- fun, bubbly, full of energy + up beat is a must **
- has a positive outlook on life
- encouraging
- creative (lots of ideas + up for trying new things)
- imaginative (Shanni loves imaginative play for all things fantasy)
- patient, non judgement + won't hold grudges
- CALM. tone of voice + approach. Give Shanni boundaries in a respectful, calm way.

Getting To Know You, Getting To Know All About You

When Helen's daughter, Laura, was six, she started to say that she did not want to go to school and that she was scared of her teacher. She had been told off for not having the right clothes for sports. Helen went to meet the teacher, who said that she had not really been able to get to know Laura, as she is quiet in class. She had not told Laura off about clothes for sports, but had pointed out that if she only had shorts, and not jogging bottoms, then her legs would get cold.

Helen and Andy decided that they needed to help the teacher to learn more about Laura - and quickly. Helen talked to Laura and got some ideas together as a sort of profile of her. Over Christmas, when they were with their extended family, Laura showed the profile to each individual family member and they added their views. It was lovely for Laura to hear what her family likes and admires about her. Then, after Christmas, over a hot chocolate in a café, Laura and Helen thought about what information to keep in and what to leave out. They shared it with the teacher after school.

'This would have been very useful to have had at the beginning of the year,' she said. She talked about how helpful this information would be at some of the important transition times, like children coming from nursery into school, and moving from class to class.

Laura's one-page profile (on the following page) is used to help her transition from class to class. Laura, her parents and her teacher update the information at the end of each school year. The information on the page is moved to one side of the page, leaving the right side blank. Laura, her parents and the teacher all write on the blank side what they have learned or noticed about Laura over the year. The plan is updated with this information, and Laura draws a new picture for her plan each year. The teacher sends this to Laura's next teacher with other relevant information. Teachers have commented on how it helps them to get to know and understand Laura better, and this makes a huge difference to Laura settling into her new school year.

Charlotte used the same approach and produced a one-page profile with her son Cameron.

Cameron

Charlotte says: 'Cameron started school April 2003, settled in happily and enjoyed playing with his mates. Reception year went by fine but during Year 1, the teacher started to notice that he was easily distracted and although he was enjoying school, getting him to stick to anything was hard. He liked playing and telling jokes to his friends, but the class teacher felt that as he was summer-born and young, perhaps he wasn't quite ready to learn yet. Lots of children do

LAURA

WHAT OTHERS LIKE ABOUT ME, AND WHAT I LIKE ABOUT MYSELF

Artistic, Caring, Good at climbing, gives great cuddles
Good at making, drawing and building stuff
Creative, Thoughtful, Adventurous

WHAT IS IMPORTANT TO ME

- Having 2 cats - Emily and Jess
- My three stick insects, and seeing if their eggs hatch
- Playing with my friends - Emily, Abbie, Eleanor and Caitlin
- Seeing my cousins , Honor and Phoebe
- Going to Oasis every year with Granny, Aunty Wendy, Uncle Dave, Aunty Clare and Uncle Miguel
- My art box-and doing art at home several times a week
- My yellow teddy, Sunny, who sleeps on my bed
- Knowing what is going to happen each day, and planning ahead for special things like my birthday (I like to plan my party about 4 months in advance!)

HOW TO SUPPORT LAURA

- Laura is sensitive and perceives a small negative comment as a big telling off
- Laura needs lots of praise and encouragement
- Laura does not like change very much and particularly needs lots of reassurance about changing classes
- Laura can seem quiet and shy before you get to know her, she may need you to initiate conversations

Thank you to Granny, Aunty Wendy, Uncle Dave, Aunty Clare, and Uncle Miguel for helping Laura, Mummy and Daddy to write Laura's plan for school

things like reverse letters, but bit-by-bit I became more and more suspicious. He was fairly chaotic in how he went about life and continually did things like put his shoes and clothes on the wrong way round. He told me he wasn't interested in reading, as by the time he had worked out what the letter sound was he had forgotten the word anyway, let alone the sentence.'

School were positive and said they expected Cameron would catch up and that he was happy and popular.

In Year 2, Charlotte became convinced that something more was going on and asked to see the SENCO (Special Educational Needs Co-ordinator). She was keen to see that everyone understood the whole picture; it wasn't just an issue of phonetics or visual memory but his attitude to school and his confidence in his abilities. She couldn't work out why such a curious, interested, questioning and, by all appearances, bright child was becoming so uninterested in going to school.

The SENCO agreed and said that she thought he was probably dyslexic and the school could maybe provide a couple of hours a week extra support for reading.

Charlotte wasn't entirely convinced. She wanted to make sure that there was more focus on specific things in class and in a way that made sense to Cameron, not just taking him away from his lessons for a couple of hours a week.

Like Laura's mother, Charlotte wrote a one-page profile of Cameron. Her intention was to make sure that the whole picture was shared with teachers and anyone else involved, and that people remembered and celebrated the things that were great about her son. She found a dyslexia tutor for him and shared the one-page profile. Based on the mention of loving chocolate and sweets in this profile, the dyslexia tutor set a target with Cameron: for every 10 pieces of work he did at home to bring back to their lessons together, he would get a chocolate reward. She also spoke to the head teacher who was very positive and added the IEP (Individual Educational Plan) targets to the action plan. Also one of the LSAs (Learning Support Assistant) is now training to work with dyslexic pupils and the Chair of Governors is working towards the school obtaining Dyslexia-Friendly School status.

Around this time, Charlotte made up a story to help Cameron understand his dyslexia: 'This was the story that I told my son Cameron to help explain what dyslexia means and why he has been struggling at school. I wanted to make sure he understood that it was about a difference in how he learns, remembers information and organises himself. I wanted him to know that he would be able to learn lots of things at school but that we needed to find different ways to help him learn and keep him interested and that there were some positive things about his Dyslexia, even though it means he is going to have to worker harder at his education than others.'

Sidney

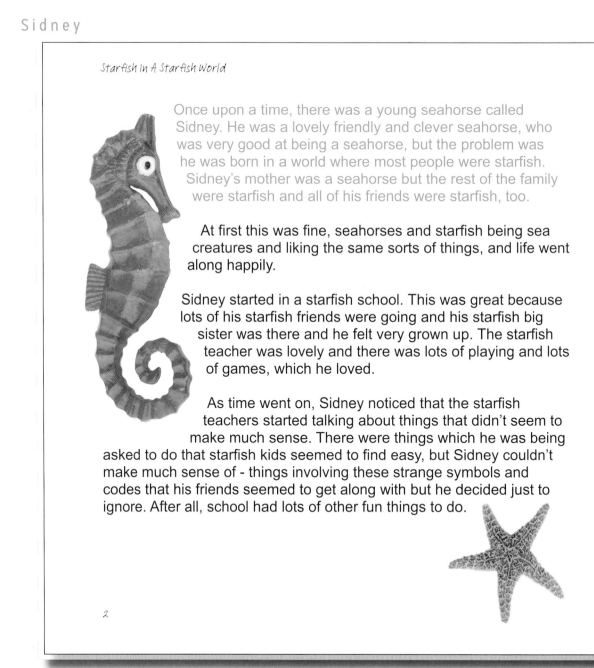

Starfish In A Starfish World

Once upon a time, there was a young seahorse called Sidney. He was a lovely friendly and clever seahorse, who was very good at being a seahorse, but the problem was he was born in a world where most people were starfish. Sidney's mother was a seahorse but the rest of the family were starfish and all of his friends were starfish, too.

At first this was fine, seahorses and starfish being sea creatures and liking the same sorts of things, and life went along happily.

Sidney started in a starfish school. This was great because lots of his starfish friends were going and his starfish big sister was there and he felt very grown up. The starfish teacher was lovely and there was lots of playing and lots of games, which he loved.

As time went on, Sidney noticed that the starfish teachers started talking about things that didn't seem to make much sense. There were things which he was being asked to do that starfish kids seemed to find easy, but Sidney couldn't make much sense of - things involving these strange symbols and codes that his friends seemed to get along with but he decided just to ignore. After all, school had lots of other fun things to do.

2

The starfish teacher thought that maybe, because Sidney was young, he would catch up when he was ready to stop playing and start learning. He didn't, though, and he got more and more behind his friends.

His seahorse Mummy, recognising some of the problems that she had had when she was little, decided to find out what was going on. She discovered that seahorses learn in very different ways from starfish. She saw that although her little seahorse was curious, bright and very creative, he just couldn't remember the things he was being taught. There was too much going on at the same time and everything just got muddled in his head and made no sense.

'Seahorses,' his Mummy told Sidney, 'like to learn in different ways from starfish, ways that make much more sense to seahorses. Because of this, your family and your starfish teachers are gong to make sure that you can use these approaches. We're going to make sure you can learn just as well as the starfish kids in your class.'
Sidney's mother discovered that there are seahorse teachers specially trained to give extra help to seahorses. This was an enormous relief, as Sidney was starting to feel like he was a very bad starfish.

'So you see, Sidney,' his Mummy told him, 'you and I and the people around you need to find ways to understand the starfish world in which you live. And always remember this: the important thing is not to try to be a good starfish. Just be the really great seahorse you are.'

3

When they saw Cameron's one-page profile - coming up on the following page - a number of parents at his school were keen to have something similar for their kids, too. Charlotte also has a scrapbook version of the profile which is at the end of this chapter.

It made sense for Shannon, Laura, Cameron and Josh's mothers to write down both what they liked about, and what was important to, their children, and to record the best ways to look after them. It sounds simple, but often we don't do it.

When you read their stories, you first learn about positive qualities, but facing things we do not like about our children is crucial too, particularly when communicating with other people who are going to take on the caring role. Admitting to have less than perfect children can be painful at times, but acknowledging problem areas and, from your own experience, describing what works - and what doesn't - could prevent a lot of misunderstandings and hurt. Laura saw her teacher's comments about sports as criticism, whilst the teacher saw it as guidance. Small communication problems of this kind can build up to critical incidents and may even lead to school refusal.

Flo's one page profile was created to help communication between Flo's parents, Anna and Ian, and the professionals working with the family. Flo is four months old, a beautiful baby with a gorgeous giggle. Having downs syndrome means that Flo needs extra support in some areas of her life. Anna and Ian are determined that Flo will go to the same nursery and school as her brother Thomas, and eventually will have an individual budget to buy in any support she needs as she grows into adulthood. The one page profile captures information about Flo, and at the bottom of the page it describes how the family want to be supported by the professionals who work with them.

Even when you spend time learning about what really matters to your child, it does not mean that they can automatically have it. It is so important to balance what matters to the child with what you, as their mother, know they need to be healthy, safe and well - emotionally and physically. That awesome responsibility again: how we can support and shape our children's behaviour in ways that will give them the best chances as adults. Some parents act as servants, satisfying every whim of their small masters. Instead we see parents as coaches for life.

The parents who tell their stories in this chapter clearly found writing things down helpful, and, to make sure you are balancing what matters to everyone, not just the kids, this is something for all of the family to do together. We also think it's important to remember to balance time with your kids, time for yourself and time with your other half. As far as the latter goes, we once heard someone say that one of the best things you can do for your

CAMERON

What We Like And Admire About Cam

He's happy-go-lucky and optimistic, inquisitive, generous, helpful. There's not a bad bone in his body. He makes me laugh. He gives great cuddles. He's a dude.

What Is Important To Cam

- Having sweets, chocolates and treats often. His after-school snack.
- Having people to play with all the time; his big sister and little sister, his mates Will, Fin and Alec.
- Doing manly things with his Dad; chopping wood, outdoor stuff, playing cricket, football.
- Experimenting, building Lego, learning in a hands on way, preferably in as messy a way as possible. Science stuff, asking lots and lots of questions.
  - Art, the messier the better. Especially painting and glueing.
  - Having stories read to him - story tapes (not having to do the reading all the time).
  - Being in clubs at home and school. Sports club, Cubs - not being bored with nothing to do.
  - Just mooching about at the weekend, playing with his chickens, roaming about in the field at Will's house, trampolining and playing on the computer.

How To Support Cam

- Cam struggles to remember long sequences and instructions. Keep instructions direct and simple. He can be really chaotic in a task; help him to work out for himself what order he needs to do things in.
- Do plans, timetables, maps - things he can see the sequences in - rather than relying just on his auditory memory. Include things he can touch, see, hear, taste etc.
- He asks lots and lots of questions. Take time to make sure he understands things properly. Sometimes he doesn't use the right questions. Take time to find out what he really wants to know.
- Don't rush him to answer; when under pressure, he struggles to find the words and explain himself well.
- Make sure he can see the point of what he is doing. He will find 101 other things to do if he can't quite get what you want him to do. Check that he understands; don't assume.
- We talk about Dyslexia being a reason and not an excuse. Don't let Cammy say he can't do it because he is dyslexic but help him to see that he can do it and give him as much praise and encouragement as you can.
  - Remember he has to work harder than most to learn school things and he can get really tired. After a long day at school, he will need time to burn off energy and will sometimes struggles to concentrate.
  - Remember that his ability to concentrate can vary hugely from day to day and even moment to moment. Make sure there are as few distractions as possible when working.

Cammy and his Mum put this plan together, with help from his sisters and Dad, his previous and current teacher and his dyslexia teacher .

What we love about Flo

- She is beautiful - she has beautiful hair, eyes and smile.
- She has a gorgeous giggle.
- She is content and patient - she rarely gets upset and when she does you know there is something missing!
- She is cuddly - she grips like a koala bear!
- She is observant and alert.
- She is a chatterbox, is always making noises and responds to people she knows making lots of different sounds.
- She sleeps through the night!
- She has a great sense of humour - she loves being tickled and bounced on Mummy's and Daddy's bed.
- She's tough! She takes her brother Thomas' 'rough and tumble' all in her stride!

Flo

What is important to Flo?

- Being massaged and stroked on her face - particularly her nose and cheeks.
- Being cuddled by people she knows, including being cuddled and kissed by Thomas!
- Playing under her baby gym every day, particularly playing with the colourful rattle with beads on it. Flo also loves to grab hold of and shake the soft toys that dangle down from the gym.
- Being sung to. She likes most songs but her favourites are 'Twinkle twinkle little star' and 'We went to the Animal Fair'. Flo has also started to do some of the Twinkle Twinkle actions and Thomas enjoys joining in.
- Having raspberries blown on her tummy.
- Being bounced on her parents and grandparents knees.
- Sparkly things - like the butterflies above her changing station.
- Contrast in colours - for example Grandma's and Granddad's beams in their house!
- Following people as they move around.
- Being talked to.
- Watching and listening to her brother Thomas' noisy play.
- Watching other children play including Flo's and Tom's cousins Lucy and Charlie and Thomas and his friends.
- Being out and about, particularly busy places like the café in Marks and Spencer!
- Splashing and relaxing in the bath.
- Going to 'Rhythm Time' with Thomas and his friends on a Tuesday afternoon. Flo listens to the songs and shakes rattles!
- Looking at colourful books.

How to look after Flo

Flo has low muscle tone and we do exercises with her legs and arms every day (moving them for her). She is also put on her tummy everyday (sometimes with a rolled up muslin square underneath her) and we encourage her to lift her head up.

She rarely cries, and if she does, it usually means that she is tired and needs to be put down in her cot and left, gets bored, has a dirty nappy or if she wants a bottle earlier than usual.

To have a bottle ever 3 hours - she drinks between 5 and 7 ounces.

She sometimes has reflux problems and needs to be handled gently after a feed and properly winded (kept upright). She sometimes becomes constipated, and may need very diluted orange juice.

To have her nappy changed before every feed (unless it is obvious that she needs a change before this!). She gets upset if she has a dirty nappy.

Her right eye gets sticky and must be cleaned with cooled boiled water as and when needed. Sometimes it helps to gently massage Flo underneath her eye with circular movements to help unblock the tear duct.

Flo has her last feed between 8 and 9pm, and this is a great time for her parents to have individual time with her.

Flo needs to be kept stimulated as she can get bored quickly. She needs to have a change of scenery and/or toys. This can vary but she tends to enjoy things for up to half an hour and unless she is happy, we would move on to something new, such as a different play gym or we would go for a walk.

When you are with us please do not...

Refer to Flo or other children as 'downs'.

Use jargon.

Make assumptions that information you have about us has been shared with us.

When you are with us please...

Let's keep focused on Flo and what will help her and us.

Know that we want Flo to do what she wants in life and to be given every opportunity to achieve her full potential – starting now!

Be specific about what support you can offer and how we will know if this has been successful.

Help us with information that we can put in this plan.

Share what we are all doing so that we can work seamlessly towards our goals with Flo.

Give us a copy of any paperwork as we may find it difficult to remember all the information we are given.

Give us time to think during meetings, so that we are able to make decisions well.

kids is to invest in your relationship with your partner. It is too easy to end up with a skewed version of family life that is all about the kids and not much about us as a whole family - the adults and the children. Maybe you've experienced the same sort of pressures? If so, something that can help is to think about and record similar information for you as a family, and not just for the individual kids. Shannon, Josh and Laura's examples of one-page profiles have a similar structure, which amounts to three simple sub-headings:

1. `What we like and admire about them.`

2. **`What is important to them.`**

3. `What support they need.`

In thinking about their family life, Lou and John took a similar approach. They have an extended family and it is easy for them to fall into responding to individual demands from the various parts of it instead of keeping a focus on what is important to them. Similarly, they wanted to keep their safety nets of support intact. Lou and John were having a difficult and stressful time in their relationship, and the atmosphere at home was unusually negative and critical. When Jos was at nursery, they sat around their kitchen table to think about this. It really helped to think about what they love about each other. They took turns to say what's important to them, and what support they need. They wrote the answers to these questions down so that they could keep referring back to them.

Recently, Lou said: 'We are genuinely amazed at the difference this has made to us. If we start to snipe and bicker, we stop and look at what we have written.'

Another person who had a go at the one-page family profile is Elaine: 'Doing this enabled me to listen differently to my children. Clare often moaned about her brother and sister going into her bedroom, and 'messing with her stuff,' but I didn't realise just how important an issue this was for Clare until we did our plan. This made me prioritise helping her to do something about it. The plan reaffirmed much of what I know about the kids, and had some surprises as well!

It was lovely to listen to what they like and admire about each other, when usually the typical sibling bickering hides this. The kids proudly drew self-portraits for the plan, and asked for their individual sections on what is important to them to be printed out and put on the fridge. The other day I saw Oscar take a friend to read his, and proudly point out the bit where his friend was mentioned.'

Mummy (Lou)

A wonderful Mummy, Grandma, Sister and Daughter, gives great snuggles, hard working, warm, welcoming, passionate, Her magic kisses, Lives life with integrity, Enthusiastic and passionate, loving and open natured, a celebrator of life.

Jos

Our most precious little boy, beautiful, a gift, mischievous, sense of fun, gentle, sociable, clever, an amazing communicator, inquisitive, stunning smile with bright, curious eyes.

Daddy (John)

~ A fabulous Daddy and Gramps, My rock and soul mate, Compassionate, Loving, Great sense of humour, My constant travelling companion, Funny and protective, Gives great cuddles.

What is important to us as a family...

To spend lots of time with our wonderfully rich and diverse extended family (including Patrick, Rosa, Joe, Dave, Lisa and Pete, Grandma, Auntie Linzi, Jos' Cousins/our Nephew and Nieces).

We play an active part in our neighbourhood (and our lasting friendships with neighbours Martin and Kate, Emma and Gab, Tilly, Poppy and Tom, Joel, Jane, Syd and Pearl) and in our local community.

To use our consumer power ethically and thoughtfully.

That we are kind to each other and respectful of each other.

That we have family time just for the three of us - Mummy, Daddy and Jos (going to the Park, the Museum, train station, go to Buxton on the train, seeing friends).

That we spend time with our Grandchildren, Dave, Lisa and Pete, Jos' Grandma and Auntie Linzi at least once a week (having a family meal, playing at the woods, going to the farm, going swimming).

We have regular holidays, at least twice a year.

What support we need from one another and others...

- That we are always kind to each other and we value unconditional love and honesty at all times.
- That we have Jos-free time to connect as a couple - this is usually once or twice a month and we enjoy going to the theatre, walking, seeing friends.
- Grandma, Auntie Linzi and Lisa are our regular babysitting 'team'.
- We have weekly get togethers with our friends and neighbours, usually in their back garden!
- That I work with like-minded people who value social justice.
- That we have meals around our kitchen table to talk, laugh and share our day every day.
- We financially and emotionally support anyone in our family who may need it.
- We have equity as a couple - sharing the workload and childcare
- We share and nurture our time with Jos.
- Respect our need to spend time apart with friends.

Clearly, the one-page family profile can have a very beneficial effect on family life. Alongside that, though, there may be times in your family's life when you have to describe who you are as a family to other people.

Anna and Javier applied and went through a two-year adoption process. Their social worker made monthly visits and copious notes. The information was put into a report that was used for the adoption panel and then to inform the matching process. With the benefit of hindsight, Javier says: 'I wish we had developed something like this with the social worker instead of the rather official report that we ended up with. A one-page family profile would have been something that we could have continually used and added to.

It would have been great to have similar information on the boys, as well. We got to know a bit about their routines in the matching process, but it would have been wonderful to have had something that, as well as outlining the support they needed, would have described what is lovely about them, what matters to them.'

This chapter started with Helen's Mummy Manual as a book of instructions for anyone caring for her daughter Ffion, and has ended with the concept of the one-page and family profiles. The processes that the families went through to achieve their records were fun and satisfying in themselves, but we hope you may see how sharing what we know within our families can be used to nurture children and help them grow into secure adults with a strong sense of identity.

CAMERONS Plan

what we like and admire about **cam**

inquisitive

GIVES GREAT CUDDLES

GENEROUS he's A DUDE

not a bad bone in his body

HELPFUL

HAPPY GO LUCKY

MAKES ME LAUGH

OPTIMISTIC

what is IMPORTANT to cam

Roaming about in the fields at Will's house, TRAMPOLING and playing on the computer. Experimenting, building lego, LEARNING in a hands-on messy way. Art, the MESSIER the better. Especially painting and gluing.

Having STORIES read to him, story tapes not having to do reading all the time. Science stuff asking LOTS of questions. Just mooching about at the weekend PLAYING with his chickens. His big sister, his little sister, his MATES Will Fin and Alec. Having sweets, chocolates and treats OFTEN. His after school snack. Doing manly things with his DAD chopping wood, outdoor stuff, playing cricket, football. Having people to PLAY with all the time. Being in clubs at home and school. Sports clubs, CUBS. Not being bored with nothing to do.

remember he can really get tired. He had to work harder than most to learn at school especially after a long day at school, he will need time to burn off energy and sometimes struggles to concentrate.

do plans, timetables, maps, things he can see in sequence in rather than relying just on his auditory memory. include things he can touch, see, hear and taste.

don't rush him to answer, he struggles to find the words and explain himself well when under pressure.

we talk about dyslexia being a reason and not an excuse, don't let cammy say he can't do it because he is dyslexic but help him to see that he can do it, give him plenty of praise and encouragement.

he asks LOTS of questions to make sure he really understands thing properly. sometimes he doesn't use the right questions. take time to find out what he really wants to know.

remember that his ability to concentrate can vary hugely from day to day and even moment to moment. make sure there are as few distractions as possible when working.

make sure he can see the point of what he is doing, he will find lots other things to do if he can't quite get what you want him to do. decide he understands don't assume.

How to support CAM

cam struggles to remember long sentences and instructions. keep instructions direct and simple. he can be really chaotic in a task, help him to work out for himself what order things need to be in.

Chapter 3

Appreciating Each Other

Big Brother 2007 made minor celebrities of 18-year-old twins who had to be taught to boil an egg and learn how to change a duvet cover. Maybe it's a case of 'You're only young once' but we worry about a society that encourages pre-pubescent girls to strut their stuff in boob tubes, rah-rah skirts and an array of cosmetics designed to enhance their attractiveness to - whom? Is this the same society that so fears and yet is obsessed with paedophilia? Maybe you recognise some contradictions here?

Being young is a stage, yes, and let's make it fun, certainly, but also safe and a solid preparation for life beyond childhood. We think this is the great commission for families, the vital undertaking in which the family can excel.

In magazine polls about what makes for healthy relationships, being valued in your own right comes out top. 'Being valued in your own right' might be paraphrased as having a healthy self-concept and anyone with a strong, positive sense of their identity might have a chance of being secure in and appreciated for who they are. And maybe, just maybe, have a chance of being able to withstand some of the worst aspects of social pressure to conform to market values. The implications for parenting are obvious.

Jake's Mum, Michelle, works for an organisation that appreciates her. At Christmas she was given an embroidered star with one thing that the team values and appreciates about her sewn onto each point and her name in the middle. She took it home and showed it to her ten-year-old son Jake, explaining what each of the appreciations meant.

'Can I have one about me?' Jake asked.

Over breakfast the next day, Michelle asked Jake what he likes about himself, and what he thinks he is good at. She told him all the things that she appreciated about him, and they created a list together. Michelle phoned Jake's sister, Tabatha, who is 20 and was at work. She texted three things that she liked about Jake and followed this with, 'What do you appreciate about me? Can I have one?'

Michelle asked two of Jake's friends, Andy and Julie, what they appreciated about him. They looked surprised. 'What d'ya mean?' asked Julie. She thought about it and said, 'He's funny.'

Andy said, 'He's my best mate.'

And they both asked, 'What do you like about me?'

Jake's final list had seventeen appreciations. Jake underlined his favourites.

GOOD SENSE OF HUMOUR,

ENTHUSIASTIC,

THOUGHTFUL,

CUDDLY,

HAPPY,

GOOD AT HIDING,

GOOD LOOKING,

FAST RUNNER,

INNOCENT,

LOVES ANIMALS,

GOOD FOOTBALLER,

GOOD FRIEND,

POPULAR,

A ROCKER,

WATER BABY,

FUNNY,

BEST FRIEND.

Jake did not want these recorded on a 'girly star'; he wanted something else. As he is a huge Liverpool football fan, Michelle thought of a football shirt.

Now Jake has a framed football shirt, in the Liverpool strip, with his name on the back, and underneath this, what people appreciate about him.

Jake, his friends and his sister all wanted to hear, and to have recorded, what people like and admire about them. It is unusual to be so explicit about what we value about other people. Perhaps this is because our culture is more negative than positive. Being positive is regarded as not understanding the real world. Talking positively about yourself is misinterpreted as a sign of egomania - you're 'full of yourself' or 'big-headed', and, of course, talking positively about your children is simply bragging.

Our society encourages self-criticism without an equal encouragement to appreciate what is good in each of us. Speaking positively doesn't belong to the world of psychobabble, though. On the contrary, research tells us that appreciating each other more will make a difference to all of our relationships. For instance, researchers in Seattle have found that healthy, lasting relationships have a ratio of five positive interactions to every one negative interaction. Many of us are not hard-wired to be that positive, and have to work at it. It is much more natural to hear criticism and correction come from our mouths than appreciations and positivity, and, like Lynda in the story below, we may want to focus on telling our children what we appreciate about them.

'You Like My Sisters More Than Me!'

Rosie was cross with her Mum, Lynda. For Lynda, this was like a knife to her heart.
At five, Rosie was the youngest of three girls, each equally loved, but Rosie was cross and wanted to make sure her Mum knew it.

Lynda thought about this. She regularly told her girls how much she loved them, made sure she had individual time with them, took Rosie to violin lessons, cooked with her... What more could she do?

Then she realised that she had never specifically told Rosie exactly what she loved about her. Perhaps just saying, 'Mummy loves you' was not enough. She decided that rather than just telling Rosie what she loved and appreciated about her, she would record it.

One Saturday afternoon, Rosie and her Mum spent a couple of hours on the computer together. Lynda told Rosie all the qualities that she liked and admired about her, and what she was good at. Rosie added what she thought she was good at. To illustrate this, they scoured family photos and created a poster together. Rosie chose the colours and the design. She was delighted with the finished result, and immediately wanted it up in her bedroom. Not only does Rosie have something that affirms who she is in her mother's eyes, but Lynda has a reminder to make sure that she tells Rosie, specifically and regularly, what she appreciates about her.

Why Is This So Important?

In *The Secret of Happy Children*, Stephen Biddulph tells us that a child's mind is full of questions. The greatest questions are:

Who am I?

What kind of person am I?

Where do I fit in?

'These are questions of identity,' Stephen Biddulph argues, 'questions that shape our lives as adults. Children are deeply affected by statements beginning with You are... Whether the message is You are so lazy! or You're a great kid! these statements from the important 'big people' will go deeply and firmly into the child's consciousness.'

If we think back to the You are... statements that you heard as a child, some of these messages may still feel as if they are etched on your mind - and they're more likely to be negative than positive.

Not only can it be a struggle to be appreciative, whenever someone dares to say something complimentary, chances are we will downplay, dismiss or rebuff it.

'Oh - this old thing? Flattery will get you nowhere!'

Yet real appreciation is not flattery; it is genuine, and not fuelled by any desire to manipulate. In British culture, which tends towards self-deprecation, it can be easy, if someone is complimentary about one of our children, to point out a negative: 'Yes, she may be good at backstroke, but she can't do the crawl at all.'

When you do this it's unlikely to encourage people to appreciate one another more. Instead, you could see it as a gift and try to simply say 'Thank you'. When we do this, it won't mean you're about to develop an ego the size of Simon Cowell's, or become known for being a bragging mother. If we appreciate our children, it will not turn them into bigheads, full of themselves. It will simply balance all the negatives that they hear, and help them feel loved and valued. If you contemplate losing a child - every parent's worst nightmare - you may think of what you wish you had told them.

It's not just families that can struggle to tell each other what they like and value about one another; it doesn't happen easily or readily in organisations or schools either. Simon and Teresa helped their local school to begin to change a small part of this - the way information is shared at parents' evenings.

Stars And Targets

Simon and Teresa have two daughters, Elizabeth and Kate, who both attend the same primary school. When parents' evenings came around, they took it in turns to meet the teacher. Teresa went to meet Kate's teacher, Miss Keating.

Afterwards, Simon and Teresa talked about the parents' evening, and Teresa showed Simon the orange slip with Kate's targets on it. Simon was shocked to hear that Miss Keating had not said anything positive about Kate.

'So she said nothing positive about Kate's schoolwork, or about her as a person?' Simon asked Teresa.

Simon had a good relationship with the head teacher, Mr. Field, so next day after the school run he called in to see him and expressed his dismay at what had happened the night before. They talked about how this could, and should, have been different, how they might ensure that appreciations were as much part of parents' evenings as targets.

That evening Simon and Teresa created a new kind of feedback form for parents. These new forms had a photo of the child, space for three appreciations, and beneath that, space for the three targets. They tried it out with Kate, putting her school photo on it, the targets, and three things that they appreciated about her.

Mr. Field was impressed and the new form is now being used as part of staff training and, from the autumn term, this was part of parents' evenings for all children.

Is there anything we can do in our families about getting the balance between constructive criticism and positive strokes right? Well, for a start, we could tell people what we appreciate about them.

But we could go further and find ways to record and celebrate what we like and admire and appreciate about our children and families.

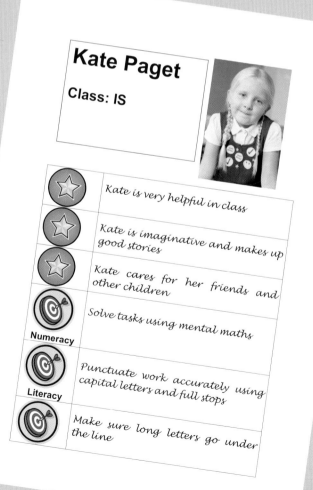

Kate Paget

Class: IS

⭐	Kate is very helpful in class
⭐	Kate is imaginative and makes up good stories
⭐	Kate cares for her friends and other children
🎯 **Numeracy**	Solve tasks using mental maths
🎯 **Literacy**	Punctuate work accurately using capital letters and full stops
🎯	Make sure long letters go under the line

'Everyday the world pulls us down, shakes us up, slices into us, laughs at our attempts and belittles our triumphs. We need to hear afresh every day a few things that are honestly good about us.'

Nancy Kline, Time to Think

Tell Your Children And Family

Think about what you like and appreciate about them and say it. Try it once this week, and then again next week – then more. Instead of five-a-day fruit and vegetables, could we go to five-a-day appreciations of each other? This might benefit our own emotional and physical health, too.

Don't dilute it, or put yourself down as you say it. Just say it! One thing!

Tell them about characteristics as well as what they do and say.

If it sticks in your throat, and feels horribly unnatural and false, persevere. Find something you can comfortably say and go from there.

Don't pretend to be happy and loving when you are actually feeling irritated and cross. Your child will know and it will feel confusing to them.

Be specific, keep it short and, of course, genuine.

Be sufficiently 'present' in the time you spend with your children to notice what they do well.

Psychologists tell us that we should praise the behaviours we want to see more of; so sincere, specific appreciations could lead to change at many levels.

It is all in the way you say it. Research tells us that the tone of your voice can be even more significant than the actual words you use.

What If Your Child Is Embarrassed By Praise?

If your child is at a stage where they are embarrassed by direct praise, you could say what you like and appreciate about them to others while they are within earshot. If you mention your child's name while you are doing this, your child will pick this up. This is the party syndrome - you know, when you're at a party and, above the hubbub, you suddenly hear your name and try to tune in to what is being said about you. Stephen Biddulph puts it this way: 'Your brilliant hearing system is filtering every conversation within range in the room and, if a key word or phrase occurs, the switchboard department in your brain 'puts it through' to conscious attention.'

Erin says: 'The vicar's suggestion changed things for me. I was at my friend Tilda's wedding, and as part of the ceremony, the vicar gave these simple, but powerful, words of advice: "Say something nice to each other each day."

It sounded banal at first, but the more I thought about it, the more I realised that I don't tell David what I appreciate about him; it just doesn't come naturally to me. So I made a list of everything that I love about him. I have had this list for two years now. It is tatty and dog-eared, and I keep it in my handbag, tucked away in the zip pocket. I look at it most weeks, to remind myself to say something nice to David each day.'

For you, the first step might be reflecting about what it is you appreciate about your loved ones. Step two might be recording these thoughts somewhere, as Erin did. Step three would be regularly remembering, if necessary, to look at the list and to tell the person what you appreciate about them. But do bear in mind that how you express your appreciation matters:

'Appreciation of someone
needs to be genuine,
succinct and concrete.
If you fake it,
they will know.
If you go on and
on and on,
they will go numb.
If you are too general,
they will not believe you.'

Nancy Kline, Time to Think

Next: a couple of quick pointers on how you might go about appreciating the ones you love.

Record And Celebrate It

Write it down. A note or letter will be kept and treasured. Be proud of it and share it. Make it public, like Jo and Steve did in the story below. This can really feel as if it goes against the grain, but have a go. This will be something that your children will tell their grandchildren about - honestly.

The Family Serving Dish

Jo and Steve had had a difficult summer with work and family pressures, and they were all exhausted. They decided that they needed to sit down as a family and talk about it. Jo recalls this time: 'Family meetings were an alien and uncomfortable idea, but I wanted everyone to talk about what had happened, and how we could help each other.

Olivia and Jess moaned at the idea, but I persisted. The children sat round the table, looking sullen. I decided that we would start in a positive way, and asked everyone to say what they loved about each other - which wasn't at all what the girls were expecting.

We decided that we wanted a permanent record of what we love about one another. Our friend Sally has beautiful handwriting and we asked her to help us record our feelings about each other by writing them on a serving dish.

In this way, we created a celebration of who we are as a family and what we love about each other. We eat our Sunday roast off it each week, and every time we use it, we read what we like and admire about each other again.'

Steve...

cheeky loving trustworthy WONDERFUL LOYAL supportive PROTECTIVE generous brilliant THOUGHTFUL Beautiful Snuggly SUPERB KIND Lovely generous

...Jo...

Why Is This Important?

Jo and Steve made a powerful record of their appreciations, which, because of the intensity with which children may hear other messages about themselves, is an important thing for a family to do.

We can say things when we are angry and exhausted in a louder, more forceful way than we say things that are positive. When Nicola knocks over her second glass of Coke, Annie, her Mum may, frustrated or impatient, snap, 'You're so clumsy.' But of course she doesn't want Nicola to grow up believing that she is fundamentally a clumsy child – she isn't.
Now, in these situations, Annie tries to focus on her behaviour. She may well still be frustrated, but, instead of beginning with a *You* are… put-down, she tries to say that it was a clumsy thing to do.

Steve Biddulph again:
'The problem comes when the positive messages, "You are great, we love you," are not equally strong or reliable. Often, although we feel these, we do not communicate them. Almost every child is dearly loved, but many children do not know this fact: many adults will go to their deaths still believing that they were a nuisance and a disappointment to their parents.'

Making a permanent record of what you appreciate about your child makes this much less likely to happen. There'll be something they can keep, and probably treasure, that will be a reminder of how much they are loved and appreciated. For who they are.

It's all too apparent that the media and marketing people have a huge influence on the social context in which families exist. They might, you could say, set the agenda - but the parents and children in this chapter have refused to let that agenda define and dictate who they are and might aspire to be. Here, they have shared a number of stories about what's important to them and how they have captured and recorded, with a spirit of love and appreciation, what they value in one another.

Chapter 4

Rhythms, Rituals and Routines

In our attempts to be good parents, current debate claims, many of us are trying too hard to give our children the best of everything, so much so that we are not helping them develop the vital capacity to tolerate frustration. One simple aim of psychotherapy is to learn what we can change and, alongside that, how we can live more comfortably with what we cannot. In parenting - where the more mature parent and the immature child are poles apart - it is the responsibility of the adult to create an environment where change is negotiated not enforced. It's known as the rule of sensitive responsiveness. It's known as the rule of sensitive responsiveness.

This chapter is about listening so that you may find out what truly matters to your child, and what this means for the rhythms, rituals and routines of life and helping them negotiate their way through its possibilities. It is about discovering what makes your child's heart sing - but also what makes that heart sink. It is about the good and bad news in parenting. After all these years, Maye's heart still aches remembering when she had to give her small son, Robert, bad news. When she got him ready for school on what would have been his second day there, he looked at her in puzzlement and said, 'But I did school yesterday.' Maye was the one who had to break the news that school was for the next 13 years. Let's hear some stories about parents responding sensitively to help their children manage the pressures of life.

Lucy doesn't do mornings very well. On the next page, Barbara, her Mum, describes Lucy's best and worst mornings.

On one level, Barbara knew all of this - all her likes and dislikes - but now she saw it with fresh eyes and got the point. In many ways, Lucy was describing the difference between a school day morning and a weekend morning. Hearing this from Lucy helped Barbara to realise the importance for her of the rhythm and pace of her mornings. She hadn't realised that she was particular about her clothes and how they felt on her skin; it wasn't just what they looked like. As well as getting a different perspective on what's important to Lucy, what she said gave Barbara clues about how to change their family morning routines and make life better for everyone. They are simple things, which maybe many families do anyway, but listening to her good and bad mornings has altered their routines.

A happier Lucy has made for less stressful mornings for all of the family. She is much less moody and sulks far less at breakfast. Result! Now Barbara is going to discover what good and bad mornings look like for her other children, and for her partner and herself as well.

BLISS...

NO ONE WAKES LUCY UP. NO ALARM GOES OFF AND THE NOISES OF HER SISTERS GETTING UP DON'T ROUSE HER. THAT MAKES IT ONE OF HER FAVOURITE MORNINGS BECAUSE, FOR HER, LYING IN IS BLISS. LUCY KNOWS HER IDEAL ROUTINE WELL:

'THEN I PUT ON MY TOWELLING ROBE,' SHE SAYS, 'MY BLUE, MANCHESTER CITY ROBE – I HATE BEING COLD – AND WANDER DOWN TO WATCH TELLY.' SHE DOESN'T HAVE TO FIGHT HER SISTERS FOR HER FAVOURITE SPACE AT THE END OF THE SOFA, NEAREST TO THE TELLY. 'AND DAD BRINGS ME BREAKFAST ON A TRAY: WHITE BREAD (DEFINITELY NOT THAT HORRIBLE BROWN STUFF WITH BITS IN) AND CHOCOLATE SPREAD (NOT THE HAZELNUT STUFF, THE REAL CHOCOLATE SPREAD) AND A MILKY COFFEE. IT HAS TO BE FROTHY AND VERY WEAK AND IT HAS TO BE IN MY SPECIAL 'LUCY' MUG.'

'THEN I GET RUSHED,' SHE SAYS. 'DAD WILL BE CALLING UP THE STAIRS, HURRY UP AND GET DRESSED! AND HE'LL BE NAGGING ME BECAUSE I DON'T DO EVERYTHING AS FAST AS HE WANTS ME TO. IT'S LIKE – GET DOWN HERE FOR YOUR BREAKFAST NOW!'

CONTRAST BLISSFUL WITH DIABOLICAL: ON LUCY'S WORST MORNINGS, HER SISTERS WAKE HER UP, WHICH GUARANTEES A BAD MORNING FOR HER – AND, THEREFORE, FOR ALL OF US REALLY.

ADD TO THE WORLD-SHATTERING CALAMITY THAT LUCY CAN'T FIND HER SCHOOL UNIFORM, AND HAS TO WEAR THE CARDIGAN SHE HATES. 'UGH, I CAN'T STAND IT! IT FEELS ALL SCRATCHY ON MY SKIN AND IT'S COMPLETELY THE OPPOSITE OF FLUFFY, MY FAVOURITE SCHOOL SWEATSHIRT.'

THERE'S NO TIME FOR WATCHING TV, SHE HAS TO EAT BROWN BED WITH BITS IN IT, LOTS OF FRUIT (TOWARDS HER FIVE PORTIONS OF FRUIT OR VEGETABLES A DAY). 'THAT BIT ALWAYS COMES WITH MUM'S HEALTHY EATING LECTURE,' SHE SAYS, 'AND I GET FORCED TO DRINK WATER, WHICH COMES WITH THE DRINKING-EIGHT-GLASSES-OF-WATER-A-DAY LECTURE.'

WHAT HAPPENED NEXT...

THEY BOUGHT TWO MORE 'FLUFFY' SWEATSHIRTS, TO MAKE SURE SHE HAS ONE EVERY DAY. IF SHE GETS DOWN FOR BREAKFAST EARLY ENOUGH, SHE CAN WATCH TV. IT IS IMPOSSIBLE FOR HER TO WAKE UP NATURALLY ON A SCHOOL DAY, SO SHE AGREED THAT AN ALARM WAS THE 'LEAST WORST' OPTION FOR BEING WOKEN UP.

BARBARA NOW HELPS LUCY SET HER CLOTHES OUT THE NIGHT BEFORE. THEY LAY THEM OUT AS IF LUCY WAS LYING ON THE FLOOR IN THEM, SO SHE CAN SEE THAT SHE HAS EVERYTHING SHE NEEDS. SOMETIMES MIA THE CAT SLEEPS ON THEM!

'IT'S MILES BETTER NOW,' LUCY SAYS, 'ALTHOUGH I'D STILL RATHER DAD BROUGHT ME WHITE BREAD WITH CHOCOLATE SPREAD AND FROTHY COFFEE EVERY DAY!'

It's easy for listening to your children only to happen when you are doing something else: loading the dishwasher, hunting for school socks, or finding your to-do list. But to be listening, and understanding, properly you need to give them your full attention. And be prepared to be surprised. It may be that what makes a child's heart sing is the comfort of a favourite teddy, who occupies an almost sacred position on the bed, or following every movement and breath of a particular football team, or spending Saturday mornings panting up hills as part of the cross country team.

As mothers, we might believe we automatically know our children as well as we are supposed to. 'Of course I know my son well - I'm his mother!' is a familiar response. However, the listening that we are describing in this chapter, listening to what the rhythms, rituals and routines of their life tell us, could just take your knowledge of your child to a different level.

It all starts with asking different questions.

Different Questions

We know the questions that don't work. In Helen's family, 'Did you have a good day at school today?' meets with a monosyllabic answer or a stare that says, 'Why do parents always ask such boring questions?'

If we want to learn about our child on a different level, we need different questions. Different questions can help us uncover what really matters, what is most important to your child, from their perspective. In each family they will be different but here are some questions we've learned - both at home and through our work - which often show a result. They can be adapted for your child and woven into the fabric and conversations of the day. But remember not to interrogate - Maye learned that when she overheard her son answer the question, 'What it's like having a mother who's a psychotherapist?' He shrugged and said, 'It's like living with a laser beam under a microscope.'

Asking About The Best And Worst

You could start with mornings. Then you can use similar questions for the best days at school or nursery, the best evenings, the best weekends. If 'best' doesn't work for your child, then try 'good', 'cool', 'great' - or whatever word you hear them using to express this sentiment. Here are some to start with:

`What would be the best ever morning for you?`

`How would you be woken up?`

`What would happen next?`

Then what would you do?

What would be the best breakfast for you?

Then what would happen?

Next, you could find out about the worst mornings (or days, or evenings, or weekends). You may not want to ask this all at once, in case it's like asking your child to relive their worst experiences. Remember that worst mornings are not always the opposite of best.

What would be the worst ever morning for you?

How would you be woken up?

What would happen next?

Then what would you do?

What would be the worst breakfast for you?

Then what would happen?

Is there anything particular that makes you sad or angry in the morning?

When you talk about best and worst evenings and weekends, here are some questions to start with:

What is your favourite way to spend the weekend?

When would you get up?

Who would you spend the day with?

What would you do?

What would you eat?

What would you do in the evening?

When would you go to bed?

And then:

What would be the worst way to spend the weekend?

Who would you spend the day with?

What would you do?

What would you eat?

What would you do in the evening?

When would you go to bed?

Asking about great evenings and weekends could tell you about important people, music, hobbies, films, and TV programmes in your child's life. Listen to what the answers tell you about the rhythm and pace of their life, the characteristics of the people they click with, and other gems or insights that these answers reveal.

As you discover what really matters to your child, you could ask questions that might help you understand just how important these things are. For example, Tina knew that watching The Simpsons was important to her son, Greg. When she casually asked him one evening if they could have dinner later, (cutting into the first fifteen minutes of the show), the strength of his reaction helped her realise just how important catching The Simpsons was to him! To gauge the importance of something to your child, you could ask questions like:

`What would it feel like if you missed this?`

`How far would you go not to miss it?`

You can adapt these questions to make them work for your child. For instance, Naz felt unable to tell her Mum about her best and worst mornings, days or evenings, but she could describe her last week in detail. Asking 'What would have made that better?' was how her Mum learned what was important to Naz.

More Questions

Keep having conversations about routines and best and worst days. Make it part of family conversation. But bear in mind that things change. Maye's Dad spent 20 years eating tuna sandwiches which he didn't really like - all because one week he had enjoyed them and told her Mum so.

To avoid the likes of this in your family, you might want to keep a record of what's important to your child, but do bin that psychological clipboard and avoid taking notes in front of your child. It's much better to record their preferences discreetly.

Here are some further questions that families have found helpful. When it comes to planning parties and celebrations, finding out what people like can be important, so you might ask your child questions like these:

`If Dad were throwing a surprise birthday party for you, whom would you hope he invited?`

`For you, what would be the worst kind of party or celebration?`

Helen, being the recipient of a surprise birthday party herself, one of her worst ever, wishes she had been asked for this information, or had volunteered it herself!

All of us have bad days as well as good and we find our own ways of recovering from them, so questions like these might help in your family:

After a bad day at school, what do you do to try and feel better?
If you are generally feeling down, what do you do to cheer yourself up?

Your children will have noticed what you do to cheer yourself up. Maye once made a rule that she would not have a gin and tonic until after 6 pm. Her daughter reported to her grandmother that one day - a particularly gruelling day, Maye would like to point out - her daughter found Maye altering the time on the clock to bring 6 pm forward.

It's useful to see what choices your children can make. For instance, he or she will have beloved possessions, which you might find out by asking a question like this:

What would you rescue if your house was on fire and you could only take one thing (or two, or three)?

It came as a surprise to Honor's Mum that her pirate sword would be the crucial thing for her to rescue if the house was burning down. However, bear in mind that many children hear that question and start to worry about house fires, so you might want to adapt it:

What would make you saddest if it got broken or lost?
What is so special to you that you would never lend it to anyone else?

In setting out to recording the rhythms, rituals and routines of your child's life, you are playing the part of private detective. You are, in your day-to-day family life, subtly asking questions and noticing information. As you go about it, you might want to invite others to share this journey of learning what is important to your child. But in all of this, be prepared for the 'I hate it when you.....' comments from your children.

One way to collect this information more directly is by using a poster, like the one on the next page, and filling it in together.

There are two other examples of posters at the back of the book which are available as a free download from www.celebratingfamilies.co.uk

Good Information

Matthew had been badly bullied at school, which damaged his self-esteem and confidence. He had changed from fun loving and outgoing to withdrawn and quiet. As a last resort, his family decided to move to a new area, and Matthew joined the local primary school. Maura, his Mum, talked to Miss Petris, the staff member assigned to help enable more vulnerable students, about what she could do to help. Miss Petris suggested that the school could do most if it had good information about Matthew.

Maura decided to throw a party. She has a large, close-knit, Irish family who love to get together and party. What she had in mind, though, would be a different kind of celebration. She said, 'I hoped that the rest of the family and old friends could help us gather the information school needed. After the difficult year we had all been through, I wanted school to celebrate Matthew for who he is.'

Matthew was cautious about the idea, but Maura thought he was also secretly pleased. They chose a date, and Matthew wrote the invitations. Maura said: 'We decorated the house together with balloons and streamers. We put out wine, cola for the kids, and nibbles. We played Matthew's favourite music and stuck large sheets of plain paper to the walls. We wrote questions on these sheets for people to answer in writing.

The younger children had their own sheets of paper on the wall, and drew pictures of Matthew or themselves with Matthew, or even his favourite teddy.'

Although Maura could easily have answered all of these questions herself, she wanted to hear the different perspectives of the rest of her family.

'I must say I worried that Matthew would be embarrassed reading questions like What do you like about Matthew? and What is great about him? As it turned out, though, he loved it. He loved being the centre of attention, loved seeing people guess what would be a good day for him and he loved hearing all the stories of the good times we had together.'

Maura and Matthew used the information from the party to put together three pages of what people liked about Matthew, what was important to him, and what helped him generally, so that this information could be used at school. 'Not only did we have great information for Miss Petris,' Maura said, 'I think it also helped Matthew see how much he is loved and valued.'

In Chapter 2, Sharing What We Know, acting as a good coach for life appeared on our list of what mothers do, and it might be a good description of the role of any parent. Interestingly, life coaching appears to be a whole new industry. Until recently, if you turned on the television you might find a counsellor tucked away somewhere; now it's as likely to be a life coach. Life coaches seem to use positive thinking to bring out the best in us. When Helen finds herself acting as critic rather than coach, she tries to remember this. Here are some questions similar to those a life coach might ask:

If you could change something about your life, what would it be?

What happens in your life that you would like to stop?

What would you like to try out?

What would you actually like to start doing?

Where would you like to go?

Record It

You and your child could write down this information and keep it as a record - of what really matters in their life, or how best to look after them. Making a ritual out of the recording can be very reassuring. Here are some possibilities:

1. Write it down - with the child's drawings or photos.

Evie and her Mum, Julie, bought a photo flip up album to create a file all about what matters to Evie. On each page, they put a photo and underneath this they recorded a few points about why it was important to Evie.

2. Use commercial products.

Some of which, like Clippykit®, you can buy on the internet and customise. With Clippykit® you can create a file cover, bag, placemat or even a lamp that reflects what is important to your child. It only took Erin a couple of hours to find photos and images of people and things that are important to her and which she used to make this bag. She uses it to store her favourite things.

3. Another product you can find online is a Clip Clock.

When Laura was redecorating her room, she wanted a way of showing what's important to her. For her birthday Helen bought her a clock that had clips instead of numbers. Laura chose her Top 12 important things and people to represent each number.

4. Ask someone you know who's arty to represent what's important to your child visually and colourfully.

5. Fill a frame.

Rachel has cerebral palsy, and cannot talk, but has lots of other ways of communicating. Her Mum asked a local artist she met at a craft fair to create something that represents what's important to Rachel. She filled a frame with objects that reflect what matters to Rachel. Just because Rachel can't talk it doesn't mean that she hasn't got a lot to say. Now when people meet Rachel, a quick look at her frame opens up lots of possibilities for conversations.

There have been lots of adult voices in this chapter, talking about how rhythms, rituals and routines matter and looking at ways that children's voices can be raised to modify the harboured assumptions that adults around them might have about what makes for quality of life within the family. But proceed with care.

When Maye's children were of an age to help out round the house, she introduced a Chore and Reward scheme to ease the business of getting essential chores done in what she hoped would be an equitable way for them - a working mother and her two kids. They designed two sets of cards. The first was for Chores. (The usual stuff: taking out the rubbish, feeding the dishwasher without leaving cups on top of it, feeding the washing machine etc.) The second was for Rewards. The scheme involved taking three Chore cards and one Reward card. They decided between them what the chores would be and Robert, Katherine and Maye suggested what they considered suitable rewards. Because they each came up with their own preferred rewards, you can see that this is an outworking of what we have just been discussing: how we can respond to individuals in the ways they prefer.

In general, what they set up back then worked very nicely, but there was one occasion when their Chore and Reward scheme yielded one of those memorable moments found in every family history.

Maye was having coffee with her very traditional mother, when Robert came in clutching some of his sister's clothes and asked, 'Are these delicates?' His Grandmother's face said it all. But today Maye's now-adult daughter is full of praise for the way their system confronted gender-related assumptions about the division of labour - how and by whom chores were to be done. And when Robert went to university, Maye can remember his shock as some of the guys he shared a house with appeared to think that toilet rolls were brought in by the fairies.

There are more examples and ideas on www.celebratingfamilies.co.uk

Chapter 5

Communication In Your Family

The parents whose stories appear in this book emphasise that open communication is vital when resolving family problems.

At Maye's evening meals, a precious time when they come together as a family, there can be four or five adults and several children around the table. On one occasion 8-year-old Katherine jumped on her chair and shouted, 'It's my turn to talk.' She wasn't being naughty, just striving to make herself heard.

This incident led Maye to introduce the talking stick, which is passed around the table at meals times and when it's in your possession you talk. The talking stick works and using it eventually makes it redundant.

What's Working And Not Working

Karen and Andrew were struggling. Karen's job took her away from home two nights a week from which she returned exhausted. Andrew was finding work difficult and spent a lot of time looking after the children. The family finances just didn't seem to add up anymore. Jackie, one of their two children, was unhappy with their child minder and hated going there, adding to an already difficult situation. On one particular weekend the frustration and upset boiled over. After sharing her concerns with a friend Karen decided that the family needed to talk together, to look at the problems and see if they could find solutions.

Karen asked everyone to think about the situations that worked for them. Wanting to ensure everyone got to speak without interruption, she asked each person to say one thing, which she wrote down, and then moved to the next. They did this without discussing any of the issues until there was nothing left to add. It was a long list!

They then repeated the same process and looked at what was not working. Three main themes emerged. Using this simple approach helped the family to look not only at what was good, but also what was difficult.

Karen helped her family to communicate well by ensuring that everyone had the space and time to say what they wanted, without interruption or discussion, making it clear that everyone's thoughts, ideas and contributions were valued, before the family decided what to do next.

Getting people talking is just one essential of good communication. The other is making sure we listen to what is said.

Stephen Biddulph suggests that grown-ups tend to react in three ways when their children talk to them about problems - they patronise, lecture or distract. He suggests an alternative approach called 'active listening' through which you would help your child to work the problem out, rather than advising, distracting or attempting to rescue them. '"Just listening" is powerful medicine. If we can hold back from putting instant band-aids on every hurt, we can enter the deeper world of our children.'

Listening Well

We know that how you ask is as important as what you say. The same applies to your child - how you ask and, more importantly, how you listen, will determine what they tell you. Here are some guidelines for improving the way you listen to your child:

We listen well when we are unrushed. Forget about multi-tasking – take the time to just listen.

Great listening is letting your child finish their sentences, not interrupting, and not filling in the pauses. Children are rarely listened to so politely.

Listen with your full attention, without looking at the clock, without sighing, without tapping your fingers.

Nancy Kline tells us to put on our 'best listening face'. Look in the mirror and see what message your expression conveys and ask yourself, 'Would I want to keep talking to that expression?'

While your child is talking, keep your eyes on theirs. In most cultures this shows that you are being attentive. Even if your child looks away, pauses, and thinks about your question, keep looking at them. If this is not in your culture, then use whatever means you normally would to communicate respect and attention.

Listen to their words as well as what their behaviour is telling you.

Be aware of your body language and tone of voice – this represents more than 80% of the message that your child receives.

What is happening/ Where/When	When Jos Does This...	We Think it Means...	And We Should...
Anytime and anywhere	Jos is clingy and talks in a baby voice. Jos asks for a snuggle (cuddle on your lap).	Jos needs reassurance.	Jos enjoys a 'snuggle' on Mummy or Daddy's lap, with 'harfy' (this is an old scarf of Mummy's and is Jos' most reassured possession) and a drink. Either milky decaff tea (in his green 'tea' cup) or a diluted drink of juice (in his blue 'juice' cup). Jos will get down when he is ready.
Mid-day and bedtime	Jos gets really 'tatty' and short-tempered. Jos is easily to tears and wants to be carried.	Jos is tired.	During mid-day, where possible take Jos out in the car. Take 'harfy' and a beaker of warmed milk. Jos likes to wear a bob hat and his coat during winter. At night time, Jos has a bath every other evening and this helps to relax him OR have warmed milk and 'harfy' ready, give Jos a 5 minute, then 2 minute verbal prompt that bedtime is approaching. Invite Jos to walk upstairs to choose his bedtime stories. Jos needs support with brushing his teeth, washing his hands and face and drying them with a towel afterwards. Jos chooses 2-3 stories, read them to him and tuck him into bed, with 'harfy' and his milk. In winter Jos also likes to have his hot water bottle in bed with him, by his feet.
Playing with other children	Gets uptight, shouts, says "it's mine" or "Patrick says he's not my friend".	Jos needs reassurance.	Know that Patrick is very important to Jos ad Jos feels a great sense of injustice when having to share his toys with other children. Encourage Jos to share his toys and praise Jos/ clap hands when he does so. Physically encourage Jos to share if necessary. Reinforce that we all love each other/ we are all friends and it is kind/ fair to share toys/ books.
Anytime	Jos is asking for his dinner or 'special treats' repeatedly.	Jos is hungry.	Make Jos something to eat. For breakfast, Jos likes a small bowl of dry cornflakes or cheerio's and a bowl of fruit cut up (apple, satsuma, pear, grapes, 1/2 banana, raisins); for lunch, Jos enjoys a sandwich (ham/ bacon/ cheese) / finger foods such a sliced cheese, raw carrot and loves mini pitta breads with (Country Life) butter; For tea Jos is encouraged to sit at the dining table. He enjoys pasta, vegetables (broccoli, baby sweetcorn, carrots are his current favourites), any meat and fish. Jos always has a drink (milky decaff tea or diluted juice/ water).
Anytime	Jos is lethargic, clingy, red faced, tugs at his hair, is tearful.	Jos is feeling poorly.	Ask Jos where it hurts, where it is sore and offer to kiss it better. Jos can have Calpol (5ml 4 times a day) and if needed, this can be topped up with ibuprofen for children 5mil 3 times a day). Jos has an ear thermometer and is usually happy for you to take his temperature. Always show Jos the thermometer first.
Anytime	Jos is repeatedly trying to say something; may get impatient with himself!	Jos is trying to get his message across.	Listen carefully to Jos and repeat back to him what you think he is saying. Jos can sometimes get a little frustrated but appreciates your efforts in trying to understand him. Be honest if you just can't get what he is saying. Never laugh at him and distraction methods only add to his frustration. Where possible

Communication Charts

We communicate so much by our actions and you know what your child means by a particular look or cry but others might not.

Lou wanted to record what was important to her two-year-old son, Jos, so that the other people who looked after him, which included his Grandmother, a baby sitter and the nursery, would have a better understanding of what he was trying to communicate. The result? A communication chart, shown on the previous page, which you may find to be a helpful tool in your own family.

If you want to draw up a communication chart for your own child, it's easy to emulate Lou's and produce one of your own.

This may seem over the top detail to some of you! Sarah used the same process with Josh. 'If someone had asked me how Josh let me know he was hungry, thirsty, tired or bored I would have struggled to tell them, but using a communication chart helped us to think about what we knew and share it with people in a way that made sense.'

The Doughnut

Fiona and Tim had some negotiating to do. Fiona had split up from her husband and their son, Tim, now lived part-time with each parent. Tim was thirteen; he had taken the divorce hard and was struggling to adapt to new family routines, having two homes, two bedrooms, and two separate sets of rules.

From Fiona's perspective things were not going well either. Tim was not helping out around the house, came in late, didn't do his homework and spent hours on the Internet. She wondered if an approach called the 'doughnut', which she used at work when people needed their roles and responsibilities clarifying, might help them have a clearer understanding of what they could expect from each other when they were together. She sat down with Tim and drew a big doughnut-shape on a piece of paper. She explained that the hole in the middle was for them to agree each other's core responsibilities, that the ring outside of this was where they could agree what was flexible (they could use their own judgement and be creative) and then the outer section was for areas that were private, and so did not need any negotiating because even as a parent she did not need to know about it.

Tim looked slightly bemused, but said he would give it a go. He seemed secretly pleased at being consulted rather than just being told.

Fiona and Tim talked about the easiest thing first - the house, and who was going to do what chores. They agreed his core responsibilities and put them in the centre circle, then put the things that he could be flexible and creative about in the outside one.

Doughnut

Which meal he wanted to cook during the week.

To cook one meal a week with Fiona. To put his dishes in the dishwasher after meals.

What to cook.

To make sure that he has a clean school uniform for the next day.

To put his dirty clothes in the linen box.

They used the same process for thinking about how much time he spent on the computer, on homework and staying out with his friends. It also gave Tim an opportunity to talk to his Mum about areas that he wanted to keep private. For example, they agreed that she would not ask about the time he spent at his Dad's house, but that he could talk about it if he wanted to.

'Using the doughnut helped us to negotiate,' Fiona says, 'and we now have some new agreements about living together that respect him as a teenager, and address what I need.'

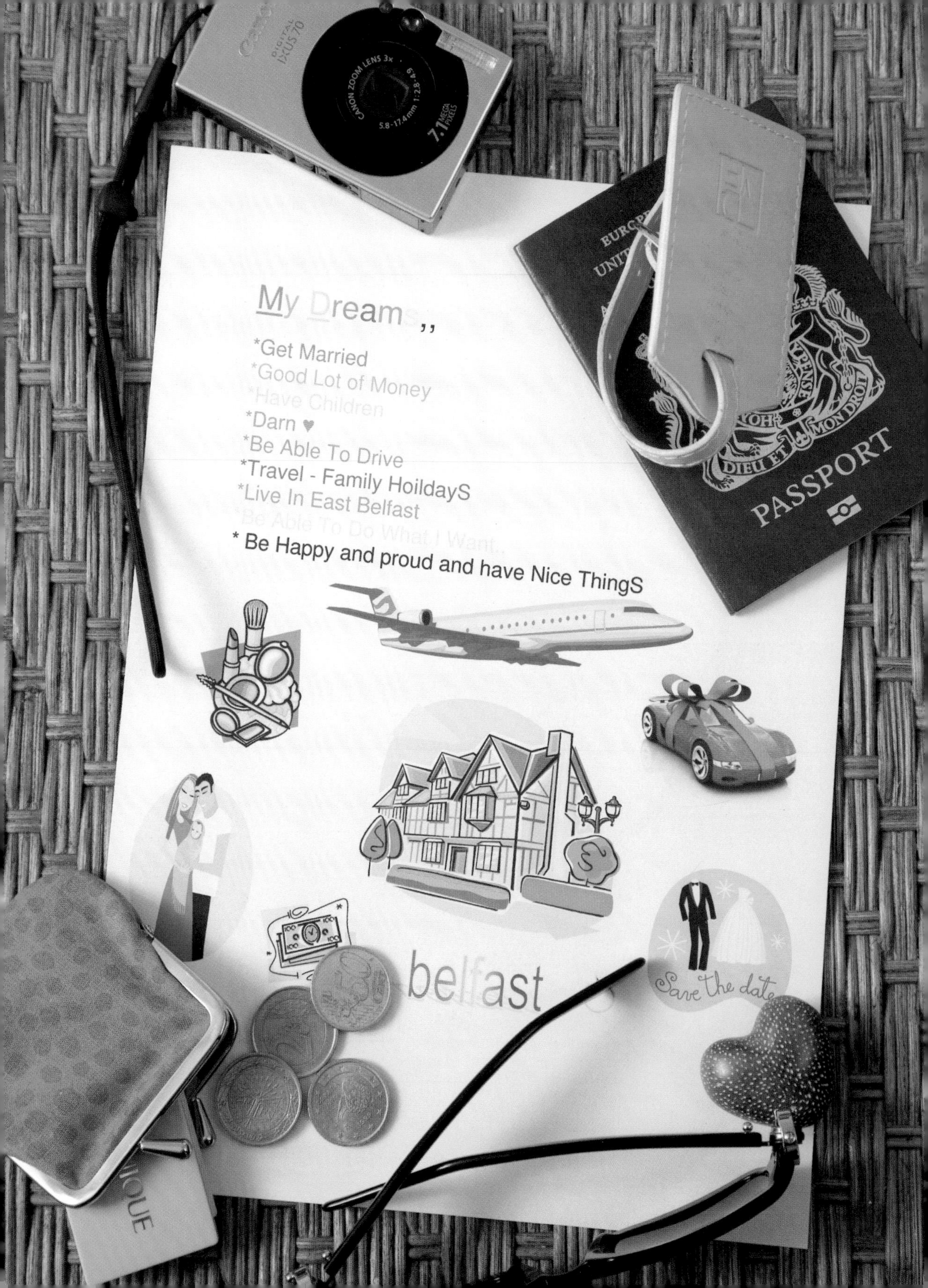

My Dreams,,
*Get Married
*Good Lot of Money
*Have Children
*Darn ♥
*Be Able To Drive
*Travel - Family HoildayS
*Live In East Belfast
*Be Able To Do What I Want.,
* Be Happy and proud and have Nice ThingS
belfast
Save the date
PASSPORT
DIEU ET MON DROIT

Evie is close to her cousin, Emma, and together they planned things without consulting their parents, told them at the last minute and assumed it would be okay. This created a lot of tension and caused problems between the two families.

At thirteen Evie wanted more freedom, so she created a page of dreams that expressed her frustration at not having the freedom she wanted and showed it to her Mum, Julie. Julie understood Evie's desire for more freedom, as she was getting older, but wanted to make sure that it was carefully thought through rather than Evie having too much freedom and pushing the boundaries by staying out later than Julie thought was acceptable.
Using the doughnut, Julie talked to Evie about which decisions she could make herself, and which ones she needed to discuss, or get agreement on, first. So they were both clear on what had been agreed they wrote it down, and both families had a copy.

We hope you will find that the techniques used in this chapter will help you open up and develop your family's communication channels.

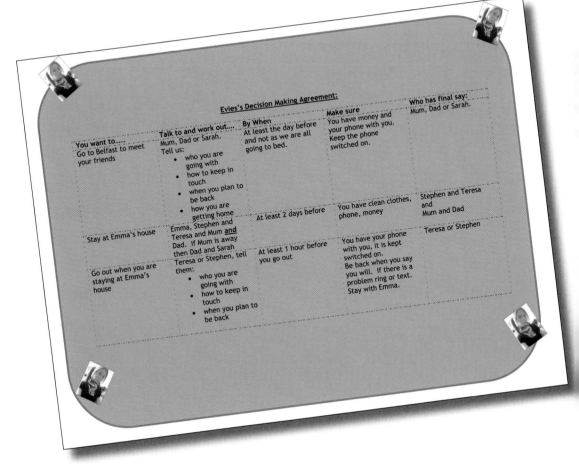

Evies's Decision Making Agreement:

You want to......	Talk to and work out.....	By When	Make sure	Who has final say:
Go to Belfast to meet your friends	Mum, Dad or Sarah. Tell us: • who you are going with • how to keep in touch • when you plan to be back • how you are getting home	At least the day before and not as we are all going to bed.	You have money and your phone with you. Keep the phone switched on.	Mum, Dad or Sarah.
Stay at Emma's house	Emma, Stephen and Teresa and Mum **and** Dad. If Mum is away then Dad and Sarah Teresa or Stephen, tell them:	At least 2 days before	You have clean clothes, phone, money	Stephen and Teresa and Mum and Dad
Go out when you are staying at Emma's house	• who you are going with • how to keep in touch • when you plan to be back	At least 1 hour before you go out	You have your phone with you, it is kept switched on. Be back when you say you will. If there is a problem ring or text. Stay with Emma.	Teresa or Stephen

JOSH
COMMUNICATION CHART

AT THIS TIME	JOSH DOES THIS	WE THINK IT MEANS...	AND WE SHOULD...
During the day.	Rubs his eyes and yawns. Starts to thrash his arms and legs and arch his back.	He is tired.	Help him go to sleep.
Meal times.	Cries.	You are not feeding him quickly enough or he wants a drink as well.	Try feeding him more quickly or offer him a drink.
Meal times.	Josh moves his head away and shuts his mouth.	He wants a rest or a drink.	Pause and offer him a drink.
Meal times	Josh cries, moves his head away and starts to move his body, arms and legs in a restless way.	He has had enough.	Stop and take him out of the high chair and give him a cuddle.
Meal times.	Grabs the spoon.	He wants to feed himself.	Help him to do this, but be aware that he may accidentally hit himself and get it in his eyes if you leave him with it.
Teeth cleaning.	Grabs the toothbrush.	He wants to brush his teeth himself.	Help him to do this, but be aware that he may accidentally get it in his eyes or gag on the brush if you leave him with it.

There are more examples and ideas on www.celebratingfamilies.co.uk

Chapter 6

A Question Of Values

When Maye was confiding in a friend about the gap between her values and those she saw around her, she remembers saying, 'All I seem to do is say no...it's upsetting'. But what message were these other values imparting to her children?

Maye still flushes at the thought of a 3-year old Katherine having a tantrum and throwing herself to the floor in Tesco, next to the sweet shelves, which of course are always perfectly positioned at the checkout. Rather than reprimand or try and reason with her, Maye lay down beside her. She was asked to leave but her strategy worked. Katherine stood up, amazed. (By the way, Maye recently witnessed a new twist to the usual 'Can I have/I want' approach: a child of about 5 insisting, 'But Mummy, I need it.')

The message our consumer society sends us is: 'My life would be so much better if I owned a ... *product*'. With psychologists telling us that we are all headed for a lifetime of consumer-driven unhappiness, keep reminding yourself, and your children, that the point of advertising is to sell products not to ensure the buyer's welfare.

'Men earn more money. When I grow up and get married, the man will go to work and earn lots of money.' Laura, Helen's now 9-year-old daughter, made this announcement over breakfast. Helen was stunned. Even though she's knows that statistically men do still earn more money than women, she couldn't help but wonder how she had brought her daughter up having such views.

As she was thinking about how to reply to Laura, her eldest daughter, Ellie, told her how ridiculous that was. 'Why should Laura expect the man to earn lots of money? Why couldn't she?' Although Helen might have phrased it differently, and left off Ellie's condescending tone, she agreed with her sentiments. Helen wondered whether it was Ellie's age - her four extra years of life and experience - or whether Laura simply saw the world differently? If she'd picked this message up from friends, or television, what could she consciously do to redress this?

Laura's comment made Helen think about the values she wanted her children to grow up with. Was she just letting life happen to her family and as a result were her children getting swept along in the flow of society's values? Was this something she could influence?

Mission, values, and success are words more often associated with business than family. At work Helen's team has been thinking about values and purpose. We wanted to be able to capture what we were trying to achieve, what we believed and how this directed the way we worked.

When Helen first read Stephen Covey's suggestion, in *The 7 Habits of Highly Effective Families*, that families write a mission statement it felt odd and misplaced.

A family mission statement is a combined unified expression from all family members of what your family is all about and the principles you choose to govern your family life. Covey describes how his family got together to develop their family mission statement. They did fun activities with the children, brainstormed together, discussed it over dinner and one-to-one, and asked questions like:

What kind of family do we really want to be?

What kind of home would you like to invite your friends to?

What embarrasses you about your family?

What makes you comfortable here?

What makes you want to come home?

Bravely, they also asked 'how do you think we could be better parents?' and 'in what way can we improve?'

Helen knew that the mere hint of a family meeting to develop a mission statement would be greeted with a look that said, 'Alien, where have you left your spaceship?' so she decided to opt for casual conversation at meals or in the car en route to music lessons and the gym. She started with her partner, Andy.

They thought about what their family was like and how they wanted it to be. They imagined that they had a family party to celebrate 30 years of marriage. If their children, parents, grandparents, neighbours and friends all wanted to say a few words to celebrate them, what would they say about:

The kind of parents they were?

What would their children say about the principles they taught them?

Their family traditions?

What was it was like to visit their family home?

After several casual conversations with the children and Andy individually, they spent time pulling their ideas together. By doing rounds at the table, they made sure everyone had a turn to talk. This meant that everyone had a couple of minutes to say what he or she thought about an idea, in turn, and without interruption or comment. As it's easy for the eldest to drown out the youngest with more forcefully expressed views, they did this several times. The girls told them about the Golden Rules that had recently been introduced by their new head teacher and put up in each classroom. They are simple, yet powerful. For example:

We listen to each other.

We work hard.

We are kind to each other.

Helen has the Dalai Lama's *Instructions For Life in the New Millennium* on her desk. She likes the simplicity of the three R's - respect for self, respect for others and responsibility for your actions. They decided to start by looking at both the Golden Rules from school and the Dalai Lama's three R's and how they applied to their family.

They typed each point onto Helen's laptop as they agreed it, and taped it to the inside of a kitchen cupboard door so that they all saw it several times a day. A couple of things have been added since; they are agreed with the family and handwritten onto the original, retyped and the latest version stuck-up. Helen thinks their list will grow and develop over time. She doesn't think it meets Stephen Covey's exhortation to 'create a clear compelling vision of what you and your family are all about', but it does express some of the values that they are working towards as a family and felt appropriate for the ages of their children; it's a starting point for thinking about their family life.

Separately, Andy and Helen had been thinking more about the values expressed in Laura's comment and inevitably about their own behaviour. They couldn't expect their children to have values that they don't have. This was a sobering thought and they started to think more about:

What values did they want their children to have?

How they are expressing these values in their lives?

What else could they do?

How could they help their children experience these values?

Helen talked to other people about it as well; there were several looks and comments that suggested she was taking this much too seriously!

Lou has one child, Jos, who is three. Her partner, John, also has two grown up children, and together they have a large extended family. John's roots are in the North East of England.

He is part of the mining and trade union community, follows Sunderland football club and is interested in the steam train era. At John's 60th birthday party he had a house sized Sunderland Flag with the club's slogan on it.

Lou grew up in a small farming community with links to market gardening and classical music. One of her favourite photographs is a sepia print of her father in his music shop, with Lou when she was four years old, trying to play a harp. She used to be a traveller, working as part of The Travellers Aid Trust providing health and social care for other travellers, with her late husband Wes. Lou still has itchy feet and loves to travel for long periods. Together, Lou and John support charities that reflect their diverse interests and shared passions - for example, the Durham Miners' Gala, Greenpeace and the Janikpur Women's Development Centre in Nepal.

John is 25 years Louise's senior, and has already raised a generation of his family. Lou had dreamed of a child of her own and eventually Jos was born. They decided that they wanted to create a family shield that represented their shared values of family life. Jos was too young to contribute, so the values expressed on the star represent the values they want to instil in him. Jos has an annual trip to the Durham Miners' Gala and makes weekly excursions to see and ride on stream trains. Lou and Jos play instruments together, and the house is usually full of music. Jos goes with his parents to national peace and environmental campaigns and when Lou was working in Australia, John and Jos spent a few months there too. As a couple they naturally live the values described on the shield. The star hangs in the kitchen and Lou says it inspires them to ensure that they are living in ways that reflect these values and serves as a reminder to share these with Jos as he grows up.

For some families this would not work at all, and thinking of destination works better.

Sue is a single Mum, with three children. 'I just could not get my head around mission or purpose for our family,' she said, 'but when I started to think of what success would look like for our family, well, that made sense.'

Sue lives at home with her son, William, and two daughters, Lindsey and Frances. Lindsey and Sue have very similar personalities and had got to a point where they regularly clashed over the slightest thing. Lindsey decided to leave home and went to work abroad. When she returned home, Sue felt it important that they constructively explored some of the issues that had arisen before Lindsey went away. She wondered how the family could successfully live together and how best to broach the subject with the children without it appearing as if she were only pointing out the family's negatives. She talked to them about it over dinner. They laughed at her.

'That's silly,' said William.

'We're not tree huggers here, Mum!' said Frances.

Sue accepted that it wasn't how they were accustomed to doing things. However, she persevered and talked to each child individually. She knew that she needed to ask each of her children different questions and in so doing help them to think about what successfully living together as a family meant to them. Sue reminded 10-year old William what family life had been like before Lindsey had left, and how upset he had been seeing his Mum and sister arguing.

'What things would we be seeing, hearing or doing if we were a truly happy family?' Sue asked him.

He replied, 'Everyone would play with me more, we would go on more family days out and people would buy me more sweets.'

Frances is 20. Sue explained why it felt important for them to live successfully together and get on, and asked her what things needed to be in place for this to happen? Frances said, 'Everyone would need to be more appreciative of what I do about the house.'

Lindsey is 23 and she understood that this was about her and her behaviour. Sue talked cautiously about how things had not felt right for either of them before Lindsey left. She asked what they could learn about this and what they would need to do to live together successfully. Lindsey said that she needed to have space, and that people need to let lots of things go over their head and not be overly sensitive, respect her privacy and knock on doors at all times.

Sue thought about what she needed for them to live together successfully. This was not about big dreams for her, but about starting practically. Her list read: Don't mess with anyone's stuff without asking, take responsibility for your own mess and remember we have neighbours and want to stay friends with them (there had been regular complaints about noise from the neighbours).

Everyone had talked about looking out for one another. As a reminder of everyone's opinions, Sue suggested that they put them together in a picture and use it to check on how they were doing. Producing a picture meant that everyone could help with it if they wanted to and it wasn't just Mum taking over!

One day Sue came home from work and was told by one of her neighbours that she had heard, from the top of the street, music being played really loudly. Sue was incensed. She went straight into Lindsey's room and took the speakers out. Her family challenged her on this. They had agreed that they would not go into each other's rooms without asking. Sue realised that as well as having consensus on what rules needed to be in place for a successful family, they also needed to agree what the consequences would be for violating them!

Exploring These Ideas With Your Family

Most parents would say that they want their children to be happy and healthy. If you consider this further, particularly what values you want your children to grow up with, you might be able to clarify what actions you could take to make it likely.

Our list of family values includes being kind, listening and being responsible for our own actions. What are yours? Have a go at working it out together - explore what your family is all about, record it and use it.

For some families it makes sense to think of these ideas like a compass. It can be useful to have a set of guiding principles, values or statements that give you direction: a contemporary version of the family shield and motto. For other families, focusing on the end point, what success would look like for your family, makes more sense. Whatever your approach, here are some suggestions that could help.

1. Do it together - there won't be any commitment to put the ideas into practice without everyone's involvement.

2. Don't make a big announcement about what you are doing, keep it low key.

3. Choose your time - not when people are tired or in crisis.

4. Don't rush it - the process is as important as the result. (Ask any good management consultant)

5. **Make it fun and be creative.**
Here are some possibilities that you can
adapt to suit the age of your children:

- Cut up coloured paper or card and ask people to write down their top five family values. Then lay them all on the table and then discuss the similarities and the differences.

- Find a range of postcards or images on the Internet. Ask each person to choose one that represents his or her ideal family, and discuss why?

- Have a family meal each week that focuses on your family's values. Write questions on cards and put them face down in the middle of the table. Ask each person to take a card, read out the question, answer it and then pass the same question card to the next person so that you all answer the same question. Repeat the process with another person and another card.

- Create a poster together, with arts and crafts materials, that represents the family you want to be.

- Make a family scrapbook together.

- Have several fun family meetings, with treats.

- Enjoy a weekly activity like bowling and afterwards talk about your expectations of the family.

Whichever process you use, or whether you just talk about it together, you might find the following questions helpful. Adjust them for your children.

What makes you happy in our family?

What do you love to do?

What good things do you see in other families that you would like to do?

What kind of family do we want to be?

What things do we want to do?

What feelings do we want to have in our home?

What relationships do we want to have with each other?

What is important to us as a family?

What are the unique talents, gifts and abilities of each family member?

What are our responsibilities as family members?

What families inspire us, and why do we admire them?

Thinking About This As Parents

Most of our book focuses on values; this chapter sharpens the focus. Think about the values you want your children to have and how you set the example. One way to explore this is to think about the opposite - how you don't want your children growing up, and what you would need to do as a consequence. For example, if you wanted your children to grow up overweight and unhealthy, what would you need to do? List these. Now check to make sure you are not doing anything on that list. (You can repeat this for any behaviours or values that you don't want your children to have.)

Record It

Once you have your list or statement of values (or picture of success) think about recording it so you can refer to it and see how you are doing. As mentioned above, Helen's family have pinned theirs to the inside of a cupboard door.

Lisa and Joe Bank captured theirs in the form of a shield, and have this framed in their family room. Michelle and her family drew and coloured a picture poster together.

Jon and his family created a family website (http://pic4.piczo.com/the-ralphs-family/?g=1) that captures their purpose, what success looks like for them, and what they appreciate about each other. Jon says: 'Family life today is portrayed as quick, instant and disposable. The development of our family website was the vehicle to give us permission to stop our individual busy lives and talk. Now this happens naturally. We make time every weekend to share, discuss, contribute and dream together.'

Lou's family created a star to represent their family values and hung this in the kitchen.

You could also think about:

Making a family flag.

Creating a family motto.

Writing a family song or rap.

Any one of these creative approaches is fun, but whichever approach to making such a representation suits your family, don't forget we actually need to use this record of our values. Let's look at the ways some families have set about doing just that.

Family Wall Hanging

Katy is a single Mum from Northern Ireland who moved to Manchester five years ago when offered an irresistible job with a prestigious consultancy group. She had been dating Seymour for two years when she was promoted and moved to Birmingham. They decided to move in together.

Katy describes her family as a traditional Irish family. 'When I go home for the weekend there is always a pot of Irish stew in the oven and the kettle is always on,' she says. As a young married couple, Seymour's parents moved from Jamaica to escape civil unrest.

As a mixed race couple, with a beautiful little girl, Emma, from Katy's previous marriage, they wanted to think about what being a family of three would mean for them and what success would look like for them as a family.

'We imagined a wall hanging placed in the heart of our home, our dining room. This was both to remind and ground us; what did family mean to us and where did we want to go as a family? In terms of success, what was important to us and in what direction did we want our life as a family to grow together? It cemented our understanding of what it meant to be a mixed race family, with our step-parenting challenges and celebrations.'

They wanted the wall hanging to reflect happiness, love, laughter - Katy's Granny used to say a house should be filled with laughter - and music. Seymour calls his home his castle. Katy wanted to use the wall hanging as a prompt so that, when making decisions, her family could question if they were the right ones and if they took them closer to what they knew was success or away from what they wanted to achieve.

Blended Families

Ruby and Samuel have been together for 23 years. When Ruby met divorced Samuel he had two daughters, Louise, three, and Jayne, five. At the time Samuel had joint custody and lived with them every weekend. Peter was born after Ruby and Samuel has been together for 3 years.

For a Christmas gift Ruby contacted an organisation that traces the history of your name and family, every known relative and coat of arms. They were very pleased with the scroll of their coat of arms and had this framed. They decided they wanted to go further than this and create something that represented the family - who they are and what they are like, as well as their history and coat of arms. They wanted to share something that they could pass down and share with grandchildren and great grandchildren. Ruby said: 'We wanted to create something that represented our family and what it means to us, and that would go deeper than a coat of arms. It would represent what it is we love about each other, what it means to us to be a family - our family values. This felt important to do, as we are a blended family.'

Ruby spoke to each family member individually about what it meant to be part of the family, what they loved about each other, what everyone's gifts and qualities were? This is how each person responded:

Samuel, who is wonderful and warm, believed that different personalities were what make his family special. To him, the three children were very different. He thought that as a family they dealt with difficult things and came out the other side, as long as they were honest with each other.

Louise is much quieter and wanted to go away and think about the questions. She came back to say that she felt loved, that it was okay to go away and make mistakes, that she had permission to make mistakes. She loved her Mum but had a difficult, not tactile, relationship but never went to bed without a kiss and a cuddle.

Jayne felt that she could go to them with anything, talk about anything. Sometimes home was a place where she could just be herself, and felt loved for being who she is.

Peter was unsure about doing it at first and wanted Ruby to explain again why she wanted to know. He responded by saying that he loves his family. Family meant going out and doing things together. Peter said that he knows that they are lucky when he sees other families like his best friend's parents, who are in and out of their relationship. Peter feels safe in the relationship he has with his family.

They asked a friend to help them to create something that captured what their family meant to them. The result is a wonderful, embroidered, series of images that reflects everyone's comments. It hangs in the kitchen, and everyone who sees it comments on it.

Your family mission, values or picture of success gives you something to measure your actions against.

Helen's family values statement made her focus on what her children got praised and encouraged for doing, as well as what got them into trouble. Helen realised that if you looked only at what she praised and criticised her children for, it would be easy to think that what she valued most highly were good table manners and a tidy room! She had to re-think the messages she was sending the children about what was important. As their family values statement focused on kindness, listening, working hard and taking responsibility then these are the behaviours that Helen wanted to notice in her children and praise.

You might want to try the same. List the things that you have praised your children for over the last week. When we say 'praised,' we mean thinking about anything you have done or said that would make your children think that you were pleased with them. Then make another list of the things for which you have criticised your children, anything you have said or done that would have given your child the impression that you were not pleased with their behaviour. Now look at the lists. Are you happy that the lists reflect the values and behaviours you want your children to have? Are you doing more criticising than praising? Ideally, you are looking for at least 7 praises for each criticism. Helen's family look at their values statement every three or four months over a family meal and ask:

`What do we want to keep doing?`

`What do we want to do differently?`

As part of their focus on values, Helen and Andy thought about what they would like their children to be able to do as they grow up and prepare to leave home.

Growing up, money was never mentioned so when Helen got a student grant it seemed like a fortune, and it was all in her bank account. Not for long. Her student debt soon began.

She wanted something different for her children. Helen heard Financial Advisor, Alvin Hall, saying on television that the best thing to do is save and invest 10% of your income. How could they help their children start thinking about money wisely, and get into the habit of saving?

Andy and Helen bought each of their three children, and themselves, an Italian money pot called a Terramundi in which you put silver coins; they can hold in the region of £250. You cannot get money out without smashing the pot, although once they found Kate having a go, using a spoon. The pots come with a slip of paper on which you write what you are saving for and put it into the pot first. They helped each of the children think of a dream that cost no more than £250, which they wrote onto their slip of paper and put it into the pot.

When they give them pocket money, Helen encourages them to put 10% into their Terramundi. The incentive being that on their 10th birthday they can smash open their Terramundi and Helen and Andy double what they have in it. They could then use half of this to buy their dream on the slip of paper and they could use the rest to open a bank account.

What does the way you use your money, spend your holidays, weekends and leisure time tell your children about what is important to you?

The Coveys valued the ability to survive in adverse conditions and so, to help their children develop this skill, took their family on an outward-bound holiday where they learned survival skills.

If you value education, you may want to make sure that you read together as a family, and that your children have time and a space in which to do their homework. You may even give your children a book allowance each month to encourage them to read more and perhaps once a month spend a Saturday or Sunday morning at a bookstore so the children can spend their allowance.

If success for your family is enjoying being together, appreciating each other and having fun together, then you may make different decisions about weekends, family holidays and shared family activities. Gail said:
'We always have a family night each week. Friday nights are sacred. We play a board game (Star Trek Monopoly is the boys favourite at the moment), we get a take-away and the boys choose a DVD for us to watch. We let them stay up late with us, until they fall asleep on the sofa.'

What values do you want your child to grow up with? Do you want them to be able to think for themselves and make good choices, to look after themselves and be healthy, be generous and give something back, grow up to respect the environment? Then what could you do to make this more likely? It is a personal belief system, such as the shared values in a family, which gives meaning to life.

However, an issue that is raised at the beginning of this book, runs throughout it, and has been reinforced in this chapter, is the task of bringing up children in a society whose values you might not share. Identifying family values can often mean confronting external values and the pressure to conform to them. Here are a few simple ideas that may help you cope with this.

To help them learn the difference between entertainment and marketing, try playing spot-the-advertisement with your children.

Watch for, and talk about, how marketing people target our hopes, fears and needs.

Do some consumer testing with your children, blind-testing cereals, ketchup and soft drinks by mixing up branded products with supermarket own labels. Can they tell the difference? How much does advertising influence their guesses?

Once you've tried some of the strategies in this chapter, we hope that identifying your family values will make it easier for you as a family to live them out.

There are more examples and ideas on www.celebratingfamilies.co.uk

Chapter 7

Belonging

We've already referred to the 2007 incarnation of Big Brother; in another part of that series, an older woman became the mother figure in the Big Brother house and was ridiculed for it. Because they lived as a little family group once all the 'characters' were voted off, viewers - by a landslide majority - labelled the remaining contestants 'boring'. For 'characters', substitute shouting, swearing egomaniacs. Another programme where relationships become a commodity, bought and sold, consumed for entertainment, is Wife Swap. The messages being sent out by these two programmes are the complete opposite of what we are trying to foster here. This book is about family groups working together, with each member contributing what they can. Here, relationships within the family and between families are seen as crucial for a healthy community built on a shared sense of belonging.

Welcome To Our Family
Debbie tells how Adam and Tom were welcomed to the family:

'Adam and Tom are the newest members of our family. Over a period of eighteen months Anna and Javier had been interviewed by their social worker as part of the adoption process. We held our collective family breath when their application went to panel. And let it out again in a huge sigh of relief when Anna and Javier were accepted as their "forever Mummy and Daddy".

When the adoption was official, Anna and Javier organised a celebration weekend for both their families to come together and welcome Tom and Adam into our extended families. It was a joyous occasion. My Mum cooked and decorated a beautiful cake. The girls, Tom and Adam's new cousins, all made 'welcome to our family' cards and posters. Our printed family tree, passed on from our great Grandfather, was reprinted with Adam and Tom's names on it. Their great uncle adopted two donkeys in their honour. At the party, Javier and Anna talked about what it meant to be part of a family, part of this family, and we toasted and welcomed the newest members.'

Helen's Mum cried when she told her that, after nine years of hoping for a child, her sister, Wendy, was pregnant. When Esther was born, everyone rushed over to admire her tiny form, and hug her shocked and emotional new Mum and Dad.

Helen had seen an amazing black teddy bear embroidered with brightly coloured cottons in a gift shop in Knutsford and was inspired to create something for Esther to celebrate her arrival and to welcome her to the family. As Helen cannot sew, she asked her friend, Ruth, a gifted embroiderer, to help. Ruth created 'Esther's Bear' from black velvet. The bear has Esther's name, and it's meaning, 'Star', embroidered on the front. On one arm is the date, time and

place of her birth, and on the other arm are the names of her Mum and Dad. Across the back and down the legs are the names of her grandparents, aunties, uncles and cousins. Laura, Esther's cousin, observed, 'It's a keep forever, not a playing with, bear.'

Esther's Bear, carefully wrapped, was given at her 'Welcome to the family' party. Wendy cried when she opened it. Helen hopes that when Esther is old enough to read, and sees the names and images of her family, she feels celebrated and connected.

'Friends and family are a mighty elixir,' says David Futrelle in his article *Can Money Buy Happiness*. 'One secret to happiness? People.'

We celebrate the arrival of new family members through naming celebrations and christenings, through weddings and civil ceremonies and these are joyous times. How can we keep celebrating our families and relationships in an everyday way?

Recent research in New York revealed that children and young people rated their relationships with parents as vital to happiness. This seemed to surprise the researchers. They concluded that 'happiness is other people', as relationships and connections were the most important factors in overall happiness.

Finding ways to celebrate and enjoy family and friends is important for your family, your children's long-term happiness. Being connected within your neighbourhood and community can help to develop friendships and we know that helping children to be giving can pay dividends for their long-term emotional and physical health.

Next: a number of families would like to share with you a host of useful ideas that may help you make the most of the family and the communities to which you belong.

Family Dates

Jeanna and Dave have three children. It's a struggle to make sure that they have one-to-one time with each of them, so every month each child gets the opportunity of a 2-3 hour special time with either Mum or Dad, alternating each month. The child chooses the activity as long as it:

`Isn't shopping.`

`Doesn't cost more than £25.`

`Doesn't involve friends - it's just Mum or Dad and the child.`

In case the children got stuck for ideas, the whole family worked together to produce a list of possible activities. The list stays on the fridge and at the beginning of each month Jeanna and Dave each arrange their dates with the kids.

Lucy and Steve do this slightly differently. Every Saturday afternoon they have individual time with their two children, Luke and Sam. For example, if Lucy is spending time with Sam, they each choose an activity they want to do and then do them, one after another. 'This way Sam gets to share in something that I like to do, as well as me doing something that he wants to do,' says Lucy. 'It feels more balanced - there's a bit more give and take in this approach.'

Family Time

Family Sundays

'Every Sunday is our family day,' says Rita. 'Homework and chores are done during the week or on Saturday, and we save Sunday just to spend as a family. Usually this is a day trip of some sort – to a park or museum – mostly free!'

Family Nights

'Tuesday nights are our family nights,' says Bryony. 'No one can arrange to see friends or do anything else. We have a meal together, then go bowling or to the cinema, or simply stay in and play board games. With our busy weeks, and everyone's different activities, at least I know that there is one night that it will be just us and the kids.'

Celebrating The Important People In Your Life

Albums And Scrapbooks

Most of us have a photo album but scrapbooking extends beyond simple photo albums. Scrapbooking is a way to make a creative record of people and events with writing (journaling) and adornments. The picture at the end of most chapters is an example of scrapbooking.

Even though Esther is only a year old, she already has an album of her family that she looks at most days.

Wall Of Fame

Helen changed her dining room into a family room. It has the computer, an old TV that the kids use with their PlayStation, and a big table for homework and art projects. One wall is covered with wallpaper that has a series of rectangles, like picture frames. It looks hand drawn, in fact, most people think she drew them myself, but she bought it having seen it on one of the many 'make-over' shows on television.

Helen, Andy and the girls have covered it with photos of family, friends and school friends - people who are important to them. If you stand and look at the wall, you could be introduced to almost everyone who is important to the family. It is adorned with the kid's latest artwork too. Last week Kate was looking at it and started one of her 'Remember when we…' conversations. They have photo albums too, but there is something magical about having a wall of photos you see everyday, rather than something you dig out occasionally.

An Umbrella Stand That Celebrates Family

Carolyn's family clubbed together to buy her an umbrella stand for her 70th birthday. Not everyone's idea of the ideal present perhaps, but this one has all the members of her family embedded in the design.

Ruth's People Clock

Ruth has a clock in her kitchen but instead of numbers there are photos of the important people in her family's life.

A Tablemat With A Difference

Freya gets to look at her favourite people at every meal. She is two years old and her tablemat has been created from photos of family and friends. She loves it and points to everyone, repeating his or her name.

Contemporary Lockets

Jo was not sure what to buy her closest friend, Lilly, for her 40th birthday. A friend of the family is a silversmith so Jo asked her to create a necklace with the names of Lilly's four children. Each name is subtly engraved on a delicate silver disc. The four discs are strung on a silver chain. From a distance it looks like a beautiful, contemporary necklace. You can only read the names from close up. Lilly was delighted with the present and wears it daily.

Bracelets

Susan is recovering from breast cancer and finds it hard to do ordinary 'Mum' things; like take her daughter, Erin, to school whilst still feeling so ill from the chemotherapy. Clare, a close family friend, has been helping out by picking Erin up from school and spending time with her. With her Mum being so ill, Erin was finding it hard to cope, too.

Clare bought Erin a Clippy kitbag® for her birthday. This is a bag with pockets on the outside that can be personalised with photos, images, or mementos. Erin immediately began to fill these with photos of people who are important to her. She decorated one side with photos of her Mum and family, and the other side with photos of friends. Erin loves her bag. She says it helps being reminded of all the people she loves.

Clare and Erin wanted to do something similar for Susan. On the Internet they found an American website for a jeweller who makes photos into tiny silver photo tiles that are attached, like charms, to a bracelet. Erin got a photo of her, her brother and Dad, and Clare uploaded them to the jeweller's website. Three weeks later Erin was able to give her Mum a gorgeous silver charm bracelet. Three of the charms were tiny silver photo tiles of her family, to remind Susan that they were all with her, supporting her and loving her.

Bags

Menghi had an amazing bag. The front of the bag is a photograph of her huge extended family, taken at a meal to celebrate her fathers 70th birthday. Menghi is sat in her wheelchair in a pink sari next to her father with about 30 of her family. She said, 'It is a great way to feel connected to everyone, even though we live far apart.'

Extended Family Gatherings

Caroline says: 'Other than meeting up at weddings, christenings and funerals, it is so easy to lose contact with cousins and the extended family. We try to organise a big family gathering every year, for a picnic in a park. It doesn't sound like much, and it takes some effort to co-ordinate a date and venue that works for everyone, but we are determined to keep it going. It is wonderful to meet up with everyone, and people appreciate the opportunity to catch up. I want my kids to grow up having some connection to all of their family, even though we are scattered across the country.'

Friends And Neighbours

Family Fun Day

Mark said this: 'We have a family fun day every year in the summer holidays. Three families club together to pay for a bouncy castle and some art supplies. We have it in our garden and invite the 15 families in our street. The kids make invitations, and we ask people to bring food to share. We have been doing this for four years now, and the kids say it is one of the highlights of their year.'

Beat The Winter Blues Party

And this from Rebecca: 'I was moaning about how dreary March is with two friends in the pub. We decided that we would do something about it. We had a "Beat the Winter Blues" party for all our neighbours and friends. As we live on two different streets, and don't have many friends in common, it was almost like bringing two parts of our community together. We begged and borrowed to make it as cheap as possible, and hired the local village hall. One friend had karaoke equipment, and someone else was part of a band. People brought food and what they wanted to drink. We decorated with balloons and streamers. It was a huge success, and now people want to do it every year. I was sent a card afterwards that said how great it was to spend time with people that you usually only pass in the street.'

Making A Difference

Volunteer Together

Penny said that for her family: 'Christmas was very different this year. Instead of a huge Christmas dinner we all went to the local soup kitchen to help out. At first, I think the children were a bit shocked but it really opened their eyes to how different some people's lives are to their own.'

Sponsoring Children

Tammy says this: 'For each of our four children, we have sponsored a child of the same age and sex in another country. Every month we send letters or postcards to the children with photos. Edialis is from South America. Her photo shows her and her family with very serious faces. The letter from the sponsoring organisation explained how people wanted to 'express their dignity', in photos. Marie asked me to take an equally serious photo of her, 'expressing her dignity' to send back. At Christmas, instead of one Christmas present, we collected enough money to buy a goat for Edialis and her family.'

Hearing Dogs For Deaf People

And finally Jacob says: 'Oliver is desperate for a dog, but both he and his Mum are highly allergic to them. They can manage for a few days by taking antihistamines, but no longer. So we foster dogs for Hearing Dogs for Deaf People. Every other month we get a dog to look after for the weekend, whilst they are sorting out the dog's training placement. It is a way of helping out and it is as close as we can come to a dog of our own.'

We called the book Celebrating Families and this chapter has demonstrated how, in doing that, several families have expanded the notion of what family is to include not just the wider family but also the community to which they belong. A community, after all, is a network of family units - regardless of how one defines family.

Maye grew up spending hours listening to stories about the family she comes from. There were few paper records and family history was passed on through the memories of grandparents. Perhaps, as a result, her son is a real collector of photographs depicting family events. Name one and he can produce a photograph; sometimes she wishes he wouldn't - the haircuts! In the next chapter, we're going to look at how your family may embrace its history.

Chapter 8

Connecting With The Past

Helen's Dad, Arthur, died when she was 21. Recently, her eldest daughter, Ellie, asked her if she still missed him. It feels strange to Helen to think that he never got to meet her husband, let alone her children. There is no record of his family, not a family tree or album. Her sisters and her Mum, Carolyn, decided to create a record from the scant information that they did have.

Every Friday, for several months, they met up for the day. They brought any photos that they had found and copied them for each other. Carolyn told them what she could remember. They went to the house where he lived as a child, and to his school, taking photos for the books. The three sisters are each creating their own record of Dad and his family, for themselves and for their children, and perhaps for their children as well. Helen hasn't finished hers yet, and then they will move on to record Carolyn's life as well.

Helen couldn't believe how little she knew about her Dad, like the time things became so desperate for his family that his Dad cooked the family rabbit (and told them about it afterwards), and she appreciates him more and in different ways. She was proud to learn how he had worked for Woolworths, putting himself through night school to get his qualifications. She now has stories to share with her children about their Grandfather.

Family Record

Andrea is a single Mum of two sons, David, 8, and Stuart, 10. Her parents, Miriam and Howard, have boxes of old photos and a few albums. Andrea was surprised when her Dad asked if she wanted his old toolbox for the boys. When Andrea asked him about this he said he was just 'getting things in order before I die.' Howard was not unwell, just getting older, but was clearly beginning to think about a time when he would not be around anymore. Andrea realised that she didn't know her family's history. She didn't know who the people in the photos were.

Whilst on holiday in America she found a book in which grandparents can record their lives. She decided that was the answer; ask her parents to fill the book in as their family record. She proudly gave it to them and although they accepted the book they were distinctly unenthusiastic about it filling it in.

Not surprisingly, eight months later the book remained unopened. She needed another approach! She asked her parents to bring the photos, and the book, to her house on Sunday. She talked to David and Stuart about being detectives and journalists, and their job was to help her find out as much about their family history as they could. She set up her computer and scanner in the kitchen. They spent the afternoon looking at old photos and talking about the memories they evoked, writing about them, and scanning them onto a computer album. After three hours they were only halfway through the photos, and arranged to finish it on another Sunday, a month later. The boys had loved it, and had seen another side to their grandparents. They had more to talk about now they knew that Grandpa had won fishing competitions and what he'd done during the war. 'I never knew that Grandpa was so cool!'

Working Class Hero

Bill died when he was 97. Julie, his first granddaughter, wanted to capture and explore his life in such a way that her own children and her cousins, could understand and appreciate Bill, for who he was, and for the richness of his life.

Julie wanted this to be more than just a collection of photos, but something that demonstrated who Bill was and his quiet contribution to working class people. Bill had appeared in the newspaper two or three times, in recognition of his trade union activities and also as a veteran of the Second World War. Julie spent an evening with her uncle and brother, drinking tea, eating curry and talking about Bill. Julie learned things that she had never known before and was ashamed that she had waited until his death to discover these things. They scanned some photos onto the computer to share at the funeral and Julie took these, creating a 'Mac book' that captured the photos and more. She themed the book according to various aspects of Bill's life - Bill the worker, Bill the trade unionist, Bill the family man and Bill the veteran. She created something that reflected who he was and what he valued so that it could be shared with future generations.

Bill The Worker:

From farm-hand, market-gardener, roustabout and cattle-drover in Australia, steward, seaman, lumberjack and tree surgeon, tram-driver in Jersey, hod-carrier, labourer, flight sergeant, air frame and aero-engine fitter, projectionist and; security man, to fore-court attendant.

9

Pa's Quilt

Deb tells the story of her Pa's quilt. 'I was fortunate enough to grow up within two minutes drive of my Grandparents' home. I saw them virtually every day as I grew up, and almost every weekend after I left home. I spent time with my Granny in the kitchen and garden and with my Pa out on the farm. They were active members of our small local community where they were generous with their time, skills, support and wisdom, as my family is now. They shaped who I am and who I aspire to be.

I knew my Grandfather far longer as a strong, active, hard working, man than I did as a man fighting the various afflictions of old age. Pa worked alongside my Dad on the farm until he was well into his eighties, in spite of painful arthritis in both knees.

Pa was diagnosed with Alzheimer's disease and Granny cared for him at home, with support from family and Home Care staff from the local council until he was admitted to hospital. When a bed became available in the nursing home attached to the hospital, reluctantly the decision was made to place Pa there.

The nursing home staff were largely kind and caring, and primarily doing what they saw as the best they could with the limited time and resources they had available. There were, however, many things we agonised over. Finding incontinence pads hanging on the outside of the cupboard door for all to see, staff supporting Pa to move him from bed to chair without a word of explanation as to what they were doing, people talking about him as if he weren't there and wouldn't understand anyway, and no one taking the time to make creative and repeated efforts to encourage Pa to eat evening meals.

Granny spent every day at the nursing home, from 10.30 in the morning until 5 or 6 at night. She'd take flowers from her garden to brighten the room, and sweets to share throughout the day. We'd taken family photos, and a pin-board to put them on, to prompt conversation and help Pa feel at home.

One thing that bothered us was the knowledge that during this time there were so many different people coming through Pa's life without necessarily having a sense of just what a fabulous man he was. In spite of the many efforts to brighten up the room, it was still very far from anything that could really be described as homely. So my Mum made a quilt. She collected photos to represent important parts of Pa's life - his dog, Tex, his orange tractor with the

'Watson Hayroll Master' that he had invented, some Jersey & Hereford cattle, my Granny's garden in full spring splendour, a shot of the farm. These photos were printed on fabric, which then formed several squares on the quilt.

The quilt brightened the room, and created a talking point for staff. It told stories when Pa wasn't able to tell them himself. It didn't magically fix all our worries, but we were at least reassured that it was an introduction to Pa - something more individual than Alzheimer's and clinical notes - for the nights and early mornings when family weren't able to be there.

Pa passed away after 6 months in the nursing home. We were fortunate that in spite of his confusion and anxiety, he never lost his quick wit, his love for his family and his unwavering devotion to Granny. Almost 3 years on, Granny still has the quilt on her bed as a reminder of those things that were important to Pa, and to them both, during their life together.'

A Miniature Life History

Mercia was an old family friend and like a grandmother to Lizzie. Lizzie wanted to capture the stories that Mercia told her on their Sunday afternoon visits so she created a 'miniature life history' for her.

An illuminated library of personal memorabilia, family photos and favourite objects is shown on page 105.

Mercia was born on 4 July 1909, the youngest of 13 children.

War time memories: ration book and food stuffs.

1st husband: Aubrey – Married April 1934.

Christian faith: Mercia was an early member of New Frontiers International. She attended Kings Church, Haywards Heath and latterly Chawn Hill Church, Stourbridge.

Daughter: Meredith born February 1935.

2nd husband: George – Married September 1957. The cottage loaf was painted by George, who took up the hobby after his retirement.

Collection of clocks: All shapes, sizes and glorious sounding dongs.

Favourite stories: Bob (Heinz 57) was a childhood family dog. When her sisters walked to school Bob would follow behind, see them to the station and then turn back. On his return journey Bob would see Mercia walking to catch the later train, would cross over the road to meet her and follow her all the way to the station too! Seeing an Angel: Mercia was travelling on the train carrying heavy luggage and had to change platforms at Birmingham New Street. She was running late, it was busy and she did not know where she should go. A gentleman came to her rescue, took her bags and took her to the train. She turned to thank him but he had disappeared.

Pastimes: cribbage, knitting, sewing, playing the piano, scrabble (for which she always kept the score – it was a delight to watch her totting up, she was quicker than a calculator!).

Hospitality: there was always a pot of tea (her best china), plate of biscuits, cheesecake or gateau served to her guests, and a Cadbury chocolate bar to take home. She loved to show old photographs, talk about her daughter and how proud she was of her, and share her faith.

Homes – During her life she lived in Brighton, Knowle, Acocks Green, Scayne's Hill and Stourbridge.

Elegance: She prided herself in always looking smart. Even for a hospital appointment she put on her Sunday best.

Occupations: She worked at the post office and dry cleaners, and was a full time Mum. During the war she kept her husband's insurance job going, cycling from house to house in rain or sun.

Mercia's Miniature Life History

These stories make very clear the importance of families knowing their own history. If you would like to emulate them, we're now going to share with you a few techniques that may help.

Researching Your Family History

Research it yourself from websites.

Ask the family! Have a family history day and invite people round to share stories and then record them.

Build up a picture by talking to different family members and piecing information together.

Start with photos. Begin by collecting all the photos you have and see if you can put them in a chronological order. Then see which family member can help you identify who's who, and what the stories are behind them.

Start with a structure and questions. There are several books that have questions, and then leave a space for you to record the answer, that could help you to structure your search.

Recording Family History

Most of us have photo albums and many have videos of family events. Using forms like these, we celebrate good times and record family history. There are many ways of doing this.

A Graphic History Map

Hilda is an inspirational woman who is proud to be 87 and living in her own home in Blackpool. You only need to spend a brief period of time with her to experience the joy she exudes for life.

A film buff, her knowledge of the movies, right back to the 1930s, is incredible. She has travelled widely whilst visiting her daughter Joan and her family whose work has meant them living in many different countries. Her latest holiday photos are from Hollywood.

Hilda was talking with her great-niece, Babs, about how the world has changed and her hopes and fears about getting older. What she found really frightening was the fact that her memory wasn't as good as it used to be and that 'Some day I may not remember what a great life I have lived so far.'

Babs and Hilda decided to spend a few hours together, capturing Hilda's life on a graphic history map. This was just the start and they are now scanning family photos onto the computer to create a family history book as well.

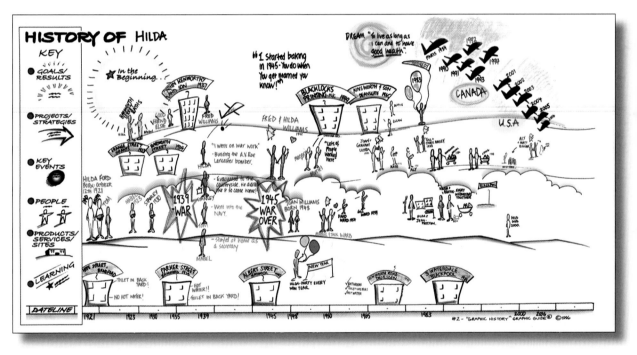

Annuals

Karina creates a specific family photo album for each year. Her children love to get them out and compare what they were doing at the same time last year, or the year before.

Mandy has elaborate scrapbooks that capture the year, all with beautiful journal entries that go beyond just describing who, where and what was happening, all the way to telling the stories and describing the feelings behind each event.

Special Books

Carla has three children and each of them have a Special Book. This is a scrapbook that has a page for each birthday, with three or four photos usually depicting their favourite present, blowing out the candles on their cake and one or two from their party. There are a few pages in each book that, as well as having photos, describes their first day at school, and a section for favourite holidays, friends, and pets. The children also suggest themes they might want in their books. Lizzie wanted a few 'Mummy and Me' pages, which just has photos of Carla and Lizzie. Jack wanted a few pages on his favourite animals, from trips to farms and zoos. Emily wanted pages on shows that she has been in, from school Christmas plays to her dance school productions. Carla spends a Sunday night every month with the children so they can add to their books if they wish.

Family History Frames

Sabi's favourite piece of furniture is her ten-year-old Habitat sofa. It was the first item she bought for her first house. The sofa lives in the front room, and above it are two shelves, each displaying about fifteen photo frames. Each frame is different. Since the birth of her girls they have taken a photo on each family holiday or get together with their extended family. They choose a frame (the more kitsch the better) that epitomises where they were or what they were doing. These range from a slate frame representing their family caravan holiday in Wales, to their extravagant elephant frame from their 'holiday of a lifetime' in Thailand. These are more than just family snaps; they are a walk through their life, year by year.

As we have seen, there's more than one way to record your family history. Here are a few more suggestions:

Make a timeline picture of your family's life.

Create a scrapbook filled with photos and stories.

Have a photo gallery of your family, past and present, on a wall.

Create a miniature history with tiny objects that represent the past.

Make an album. You could create a photo album, or an online book that you can then have printed. (You can do this at, for example, Apple's website, and, in the UK, Jessop's is another company that offers the same service.)

Collect photos and objects and display them in a box with a glass lid (a shadow box).

Fill in a family tree chart. You can download or buy family tree charts.

Maye's experience with her own children, now grown up, is that they still like telling stories about 'when we were little'. Often these stories involve tales of how she embarrassed them.

The school sports' day story is a favourite. Her daughter, Katherine, then aged 10, was anxious about what Maye would wear; how she looked was important to her. 'Why can't you look like a proper Mummy?' So Maye visited an Oxfam shop and bought a smart suit, a blouse with pussycat bow, American tan tights and court shoes. When she appeared Katherine laughed so much she didn't seem to mind the fact that she hadn't won any races.

Try having some fun - have a session to find out some of your own children's favourite stories from family history and record them. Make a life history.

Maye's children still regularly show a video of one of her Open University television programme appearances. In this, Maye is resplendent in a long crocheted waistcoat, flared jeans with stars on them, and clogs. Looking at the outfit today Maye might wince, but this is their history and to have it is familiar and comforting and, in the intimidating times in which we live, it cannot be taken from them.

Keeping a connection between your family and its previous generations is as helpful as building bonds between the present day members of your family, and it really contributes to the sense of self experts say is crucial in withstanding social pressures to be something else. The next chapter - no surprise - is about the future.

Chapter 9

Dreams, Hopes and Wishes

It's our experience that when asked the familiar question 'What do you want to be when you grow up?' many children will answer 'Famous'. Our culture promotes ambitious goals and dreams, suggesting that, as long as you work hard at it, you can be what you want and do what you want. That may promote industriousness, but we think there's an undue emphasis on making it, on getting it. Catherine Tate exhorts us to *'ave it*. At one level this is just comedy and we're fine with that, but underlying the term is rather an unsubtle message that if you want it you are entitled to have it. Our credit card society certainly encourages us to *'ave it* now; our culture promotes instant gratification across the board. But maybe we would be happier aspiring to almost the opposite.

Michael Fordyce, author of *The Psychology of Happiness*, lists fourteen fundamentals to happiness. Number six is 'Lower your expectations and aspirations', which seems to contradict the common belief that if you are achieving at a high level you'll be happy. 'Happy people have lowered their expectations to a modest level. They know that high expectations lead to disappointment, and low expectations lead to pleasant surprises'.

How can we enable our children to have hopes and dreams for the future, but not to stake their happiness on achieving them? Happy people are more likely to strive for goals within their reach. There is a balance to be struck here, and each child may need a slightly different approach.

Dreams (And Nightmares)
Neil and Alison were thinking of starting a new business. Their dream was a business that would make a difference to people, but they were concerned about the impact starting a new business would have on their young family.

On the way back from a holiday at Butlins they talked, as a family, about their hopes and dreams, and what their nightmare would be. The children had a very clear idea of what they wanted from life. Ben knew with which animals he would and wouldn't like to work! Other things were more complicated. Joe was very clear about the fact that he would like to live at the seaside, but he also wanted to stay at his school in Derby with his teacher, Mrs C. He was, however, able to tell us that staying at school was more important than living by the sea. As a family they were able to consider how they might get a better balance between those two things, perhaps by getting a caravan, mobile home or static caravan.

Spending time as a family, thinking about their dreams and nightmares, and drawing up an action plan, allowed Allison and Neil to reflect on their lives and appreciate what they already had and identify what they didn't want to lose. It also helped them consider where they were in relation to their dreams as well as how they wanted their family life to be in the future.

This in turn freed their thinking about their new venture and what were the non-negotiable issues concerning their family. They looked at these issues from the perspective of each individual and took these into account when they made their decisions.

Just like Alison and Neil, we think of the future and our dreams for it. We can talk to our children about their future and what they want to be when they grow up. Andy talks to Laura about becoming a judge. She finds this funny, but it's important that she doesn't start thinking that this is our ambition for her. We have seen parents who live out their personal aspirations through their children and this is not what we want to do!

Ellie has a list of careers that she is considering. They change regularly, sometimes in response to her friend's ideas, but there are a core few that have stayed in the running over the last eight months; these include journalism, working with animals, and a psychologist.

Meaningful Work

When Kate started school the teacher asked all the four-year-old children what they wanted to be when they grew up. 'I want to be a Mummy,' said Kate.

'Is there anything else?' the teacher asked. 'No,' said Kate, 'that is the best thing.'

It is the best thing. Kate can be a great Mum, and do work that she loves. Helen talks to her about how she loves being her Mum, and loves her job, and that you can do both. Now Kate is 8, she says she wants to be a Mummy and a fashion designer.

Happiness fundamental number three states 'Be Productive at Meaningful Work'. Finding work that reflects what is important to you is vital. In *Man's Search for Meaning*, Victor Frankl highlights for us the critical importance a wise career choice makes to personal happiness: 'if we don't consciously decide what sort of person we want to be and become, our environment and experience determine our identity and destiny for us.' Helen hopes that Ellie finds work that she feels is important, that she enjoys and that uses her gifts.

Family Goals And Dreams

Maya's family welcome in the New Year with a party and asks the following three questions of each family member. The wishes have to be something that do not cost more than a specified amount (renegotiated at the start of each year):

What do you wish for the New Year?

What do you want to do to make a difference to others next year?

What do you want to do to make a difference to yourself?

This year, Maya's wish was to paint her pink wallpaper black and have a Goth bedroom. Maya's Aunty was a breast cancer survivor, so she decided that she would run the Race for Life with two of her friends, and try and raise £100. Maya had struggled with trying to find something that would 'make her a better person'. She decided to start from the inside and eat less chocolate and drink more water.

The family goals and dreams for the year are taped to the inside of a kitchen cupboard, so every time Maya gets a cup she is reminded of them. On the first Sunday of each month, the whole family look them over at lunch and discuss how everyone is getting on with reaching their goals and dreams.

Maya says, 'You'd be surprised how well this works. I think it really helps that the New Year wishes are displayed in writing, and also that we all check our progress together, at set times.'

Dreams and wishes are not just about careers. Research on happiness suggests that rather than the commonly held view that happiness is lost as soon as you start to pursue it, almost the opposite is true: thinking about what makes you happy and intentionally focusing on it is highly beneficial. And this does not have to be as egocentric as it sounds; research suggests that if we want our children to be happy and healthy in the future, then helping them in the present to experience the value of making a contribution, of giving to others, could make a huge difference, and predicts good physical and mental health all the way into late adulthood, a time interval of over 50 years. In other words, if we can offer our children opportunities to choose to consider others now, it will lead them to happier adult lives - which reminds me of something J.K. Rowling said: 'It is our choices…that show what we truly are, far more than our abilities.'

Future happiness can begin with a healthy appreciation of what is good about life now. Researchers in California and Miami have found that people who recall and write down what they are grateful for ended up feeling happier, healthier, more energetic and more optimistic than people who don't. This, we suppose, is a matter of counting your blessings, which may not be very fashionable now, but is actually a really healthy habit to cultivate. For example, each night, as she puts Joe to bed, Maggie simply asks him what has been good about today, and finds ways to link this to things that he could feel grateful about.

Dreams, Nightmares, Promises

Nina was happy with her life as it was, but worried that this would disappear when the new baby arrived.

This story began in the autumn of 2004 when Nina had just turned 9. Nina is a beautiful, sensitive and intelligent child but quite shy and cautious, preferring not to have too much change in her life. So when her parents told her, and her 5-year-old brother, that they were about to have, not a new kitten, but a new baby in the house, the reaction was not as her parents had perhaps hoped. Whilst her brother reacted with excitement and lots of questions, Nina went very quiet and pale and quietly slipped away. When her Mum noticed she followed and found her in floods of tears, saying she would much prefer it if they didn't have a baby, please. She was inconsolable and couldn't accept that it was too late, a baby was on the way, due to arrive in 6 months.

Her Mum asked her to talk about what it was that was bothering her so much and instead of saying never mind, you'll get over it, she got Nina three pieces of paper. She said that they would try and make Nina some promises, to make her feel safer and more positive. They would record these promises on one piece of paper and sign it. The other two pieces of paper were for Nina. On one she could record the promises she wanted to make by thinking about what the best scenarios would be; her dreams for the future. The other sheet would record the worst possible scenarios - what was frightening her, her nightmares about the future. Her dreams and nightmares would help show what promises needed to be made.

Nina then talked and talked for nearly two hours. They drew some pictures to help illustrate how she felt. For example, Nina talked a lot about where the baby would sleep. She had a picture in her head that if the baby was a girl she would be asked to split her room in half and give half to the baby. She also had the idea that she might be asked to give her toys to the baby, especially Bibi, her favourite doll that she'd had since she was one. She thought that because she was a big girl of 9, maybe her parents thought she was too big for dolls. She was also frightened of getting less affection because the other children were cuter and younger, and that her Daddy would not have time for her.

Nina tended to think about the negatives in life but her dream pictures also helped her think about what might be great about the change, such as having a little friend and ally and someone else to cuddle and be cuddled by.

Nina and her Mum and Dad agreed a set of promises, such as protecting Nina's own space and making sure that once in a while she got to spend time on her own with her parents. The promises were pinned up on the notice board in her room together with the dreams and

Promises

1. Nina must not lose out on attention

- Daddy must always hug Nina lots, especially when he comes home from work.
- Nina will have time alone with Mummy + Daddy in the evenings.
- Nina will still go 'girly' shopping with Mummy and have Dad dates on her own.

2. Nina will always have her own safe space.

- Daddy will put a latch on Nina's bedroom door that only she and her Mummy and Daddy can reach.

3. Nina will have a locked box or secret place where she can store her precious things so that little people can't get in.

4. Nina will not have to give away any of her toys to the baby unless she wants to.

5. We are not planning to move house or make any big changes in the next couple of years at least. We can't promise this but we will do our best.

nightmares. A latch was fitted on her bedroom door the next weekend, with the agreement that it wasn't to be used against parents, or when unnecessary, and every few months Nina's Mum talked to her about how they were doing with the promises.

When the baby arrived, it wasn't the storm the parents were expecting at all. Nina came to the hospital, took one look at the baby and fell instantly and passionately in love with her. She said, 'How could you not love someone so small and perfect.'

Two years on and Nina still talks about her promises. She still has a latch on her door but only to keep her brother out, the littlest has access to all areas and can do no wrong in Nina's eyes. The baby calls Nina 'little Mummy' and they have a very close and secure relationship.

At the time it would have been really easy to say that Nina had to face facts and get on with things. Nina's parents have no doubt that had they taken that approach the problem would have been driven underground and Nina made to feel unimportant and not worth listening to. Instead they believe that they gave Nina the chance to feel she was being listened to as well as developing a strategy to get to the root of the problem. They also showed her that it's easier to cope with change if you listen and trust each other and stick to promises.

Recording

It made sense for Nina and her Mum and Dad to record their promises, which were the actions that came from looking at Nina's nightmares and dreams. In life and work, people who record their goals and aspirations are more likely to achieve them. Life and business coaches encourage their clients to record their goals and actions, as specifically as they can. In Neuro-linguistic Programming (NLP) - the art and science of communication - people are encouraged the think about what they want to achieve, and to vividly imagine it in great detail, in full colour, with whatever sounds or feelings are attached to it. Encouraging children to imagine and record what they want from life could assist them in making those goals a reality. Here are three ways you might go about it.

Life Maps

Accelerated learning is a structured, child centred approach used in education. It is also known as 'brain-based' learning, and includes encouraging children to do 'life maps' of their personal ambitions and goals. These can be done at home or in school. Good teachers use this approach to encourage children to think about where they want to be in 10 to 20 years time. They use this to make their lessons meaningful to the child's aspirations. This approach can work just as well at home.

Christopher is eleven-years-old. Opposite is his first life map.

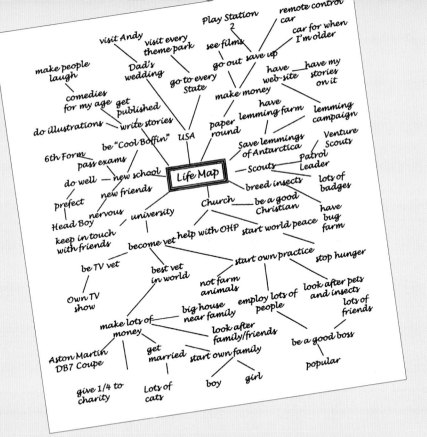

As Christopher began to consider his options, he developed his life map, making it more specific so that the direct relationship between his aspirations and his actions could be seen.

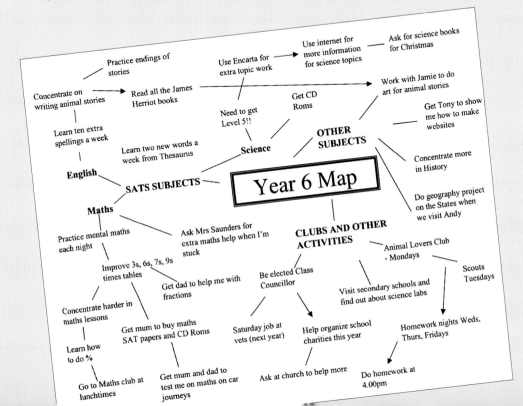

Picture Your Future

Laura drew this picture one Saturday morning. We had not been talking about dreams or the future; she just decided she wanted to do a picture about her future. She wants to live in Australia, in a house with a husband and two children, Ashley and Jamie. She wants to have lots of animals. From the picture you can see a passion for clothes shopping and chocolate.

Linking The Future To What Is Important To Your Child Now

Ellie had been learning to use computer graphics at school. She wanted to think about her plans for the future, and to practice her computer skills at the same time. Ellie and Helen had already spent time drawing up a list of things they liked about Ellie, and what was important to her, so she linked this to what is important to her in the future. Doing it this way you could clearly see the relationship between Ellie's gifts (what is liked and admired about Ellie), what is important to her, and how her ideas about the future reflect both of these.

Some forward thinking schools are using a similar approach as the children start thinking about leaving school. They have a meeting with the young person and their family, considering what they like and admire about that person, what is important to them now and in the future, what is working and not working in their life at the moment, and creating actions from this. These are called 'person centred reviews'.

Ellie

What People Like About Me

Funny   Loyal
Kind   Bubbly
Good Friend   Pretty
Trustworthy   Caring
Sporty   Loving

Important To Me Now

My best friends-Joey, Nelly, Lissy, Shann And Ellen
My cat Jess
Doing lots of sports and being on the school teams
Having my own room
Trying to keep healthy
Collecting things from foreign countries
Travelling abroad every year

Important To Me About The Future

Having a gap year with friends and keeping healthy
Going to university and getting good exam marks
Getting a job I really enjoy-Journalist, working for a magazine, designer, something to do with animals, Psychologist
Getting my karate black belt and do more karate competitions with Lissy

These were some methods to help you encourage your children to contemplate their future. Let's focus now on ways in which families explore their dreams.

A Box Of Dreams

As a family, think about your dreams. Julie's family has a beautiful dream box, decorated with their names. In it are small pieces of coloured paper - each family member is represented by a different colour. On each piece of paper there is a dream held by that person, for example, one of Evie's dreams was a huge Halloween party. Some are ordinary things that do not cost any money. Others would require a lottery win.

A few times a year they have an informal 'dreams night' when they get all the dreams out and look at them. They celebrate any dreams that have been achieved, remove any that are no longer desired, and add any new ones. They look at whether there are things they could do as a family to move closer to any of the dreams, or choose one or two to focus on as a family.

One of James and Angela's wedding gifts was a dream box - a beautiful box for them to put their dreams in. Here is the list they put in their box.

To set up a home together.
Both of us to have well paid, family friendly jobs.
James to pursue his dream of self-employment.
To start a family.
To share our home with our extended family and spend more quality time with them.
More quality time with each other, i.e. holidays, weekends away, more romantic meals together.
More time dedicated to exercising or physical activity.
To help our parents to be more comfortable in retirement.

They plan to get the list out at each anniversary, and check to see how they are moving in the direction of their dream.

Erin and Grace were starting high school and had started to think about their futures, not just about what subjects they would study at secondary school and the new and exciting things they would learn, but also about what they wanted to do and places they wanted to see. They had boxes made that displayed their dreams; what jobs they wanted to do, places they wanted to visit and their favourite animals. Erin wants a horse when she is older and made her dreams box look like a stable on one side!

A Necklace Of Dreams

Helena bought her daughter a dream locket for her thirteenth birthday, to mark her becoming a teenager. The locket is silver and when opened there is a tiny gold wishing wand that holds a minute piece of paper on which you can write your dream.

Dreams At Bedtime

Leanna asked an embroiderer to make a dream quilt for her four-year-old daughter, Sarah. The quilt captures Leanna's dreams for the future health and happiness of her daughter.

A toadstool with flowers that represents Leanna's hope that her daughter will enjoy nature, and play her part in protecting the environment.

A fairy with wishes, reflecting Leanna's hope that Sarah will follow her own dreams for her future.
A pair of ballet slippers and musical notes represents Leanna's dream that her daughter's life will be full of dancing and music.

A PATH

Jennie is fifteen, fun and bubbly. She is very creative and loves art and listening to music. Jennie has autism and learning difficulties.

Suzie, Jennie's Mum, was worried about her future; what would happen after school, preparing her for independence and even where Jennie may live and how she would be supported as she knew that she would not always be able to look after her. She wanted a supportive group of people to help the whole family support Jennie by starting to look at possible future options based on what everyone knew about Jennie now and what would keep her happy and safe in the future.

The group, consisting of Jennie's immediate family, friends and others who wanted to help her, gathered together as a 'circle of support' around Jennie. The first meeting took place in their house and Dave, Suzie's husband, cooked curry for everyone. Jennie loved being centre stage as Louise put large pieces of paper up in the living room and explained that she would help the group to think about what the 'north star' could be for Jennie and the family. She asked them to think about what they would want to happen in Jennie's life if there was absolutely no limits to what could happen...if money was no object, if anything was possible, what would Jennie's life be like. People suggested the kind of lifestyle they thought would work for Jennie, based on what is important to her now and what she enjoys doing; she would be supported by people who loved her, knew her well, and understood how to keep her happy and safe. This would involve lots of opportunities and activities outside, preferably by the sea or water as Jennie loves this and if work was a possibility that it may involve spending time at horse stables or the cinema.

Then Louise asked them to think about what could be positive and possible for the next two years, that would take them closer to that vision of the future. Suzie talked about Jennie leaving school, and the sort of college that would work for her. Suzie says: 'We were able to negotiate work experience for Jennie at a donkey sanctuary, as she loves animals, and it also enabled her to spend more time outside of school with another pupil as they both enjoyed being together. We looked at local opportunities in the community for Jennie to do art. Jennie has direct payments, which means that she gets money from social services to buy some of her own support, so the group looked at whether there were different ways to spend this money. They talked about holidays, and where Jennie might like to go over the next couple of years. Louise then asked them to compare this to what life is like now and then think about who else they would need to help them and what needs to happen in the next six months to start working towards the future.'

Louise created a PATH, shaped like an arrow into a target to capture their decisions and actions.

The group meets four times a year to look at how things are going and whether they are on target. Suzie says that she feels much more confident about the future for Jennie as everyone in the circle of support has Jennie's best interests at heart and are working towards the best possible future to keep her happy and safe.

A Folder Of Dreams And Action

Sarah used a Clippykit® folder to display her dreams and aspirations. As you'll recall from Chapter 4, Clippykit® is a range of PVC accessories with opening pockets that you can fill with your own photos, fabric, beads and mementos. Inside the folder Sarah makes notes about the actions she is taking towards her dreams.

'Completing my Clippykit enabled me to see my dreams and aspirations everyday in my folder. While I was designing the cards to go into my Clippykit, I had the chance to think more about my dreams and how to achieve them. I have a real interest in and love of all things Italian and it has been a dream of mine to go to Italy. I have a fear of flying, so I've never had the chance, but while I was doing my Clippykit I started to look at other ways of getting there. My dream now is to go on a cruise around the Mediterranean.

I have always wanted to open my own business and my dream is to own a coffee shop where I can offer customers the best coffee.

The picture of the watch is one from Zenith's Glam Rock collection. I really love the design and quality and although it costs over £6,000 I have, in my dreams, one of these in my watch collection.

Music is part of my life. One of my dreams is to be able to play a range of musical instruments. I have just started to play the electric guitar.'

It's clear to us that encouraging children in ways like these to think about their dreams is really beneficial. However, it could influence family decision-making about how you spend your time and money. It certainly did for us.

Family Holidays

In order to try and juggle their time, money and work around the school holidays, Tony's family are developing a three-year holiday plan. Their friends think that this is very sad, but to them it seems necessary.

They are trying to make decisions as a family, whenever they can, so Tony and Emily talked to their three children about how they could plan their holidays. If they save well, they can afford to go on one holiday abroad each year, plus a few weeks camping in Wales. Tony asked each of their three children to think about where they would like to go, if they could go anywhere - what would the holiday of their dreams be? He asked them for three ideas each, and for them to say which was their first choice. Tony and Emily did the same as well.

Andy, at 6, is too small to know much about different countries. Instead, Tony asked him what animals he would like to see. He wanted to ride on an elephant and see a camel.

At 14, Lucy sees the world very differently, and she wanted to go shopping in New York and go skiing.

Joe's best friend Damien had just got back from Oasis and raved about it, so Oasis was on Joe's list. He said he wanted to go somewhere they could do lots of swimming.

If money were no object, Emily really wanted to go to the ice hotel and see the Northern Lights.

Tony wanted to go to America and see the Rocky Mountains.

The family looked at all the lists together and used the Internet to get an idea of how much each option would cost, discovering at the same time, which holidays everyone was happy to do. They also discussed how much money they could afford to save each year for holidays. The family eventually decided on a three-year plan that included:

A family trip to America (that would include New York and the Rockies).

Individual skiing trips rather than a family holiday. Each of the children would have an opportunity to go skiing at secondary school, and they could choose that if they wanted to (subject to the family being able to afford it that year).

Finding a place to ride elephants in the UK.

A family trip to Oasis.

Tony and Emily going to the ice hotel for their 20th wedding anniversary instead of a party, and asking the family to contribute to this (in money and child care) instead of presents.

Freud gave us the pleasure-pain principle: humans put effort into the pursuit of pleasure and the avoidance of pain. Were it that simple parenting would be a doddle! Everyone's notion of what constitutes pleasure and pain is different and the stories in this book have shown how challenging it can be to negotiate the preferences of each individual in the family. However, that very process of negotiation touches on the essence of happiness and success in managing family life; to find a happy balance, we all have to become expert in the art of compromise.

When Maye's children were growing up, due to the nature of her work, she had to go away a lot. Attending university summer schools, speaking at conferences and working away from home as an organisational consultant brought in extra income but deprived her, and her children, of one another.

One day, Robert came into the room and asked. 'When are you going away again? Only I need a new cricket bat…'

Clearly he had learned that pain and suffering needs to be balanced by reward. Katherine had not expressed it that directly but demonstrated it. As Maye was driving back through Fallowfield, over an hour late after a speaking engagement, she did a double-take when she saw her children, 11 and 9 at the time, sitting at a window table in a Chinese take-away.

When Maye got to the take-away, Katherine explained that, rather than waiting any longer for her to come home, she had raided the family money tin and taken Robert out for a meal. They were a single-parent family where there was transparency about their financial needs and what Maye earned. Maye was away being the breadwinner and had been delayed returning. Eating out was a basic family treat and the means of doing so was available, so Katherine took Robert out for a meal. She had become expert in the art of compromise and negotiated a happy balance for the family.

On a plane recently, the safety announcement 'Fit your own oxygen mask before tending to your children', which Maye must have heard hundreds of times before, suddenly resonated with her. The message was: look after yourself to look after them. We wonder if we do that enough?

Later that day Maye was struck by a newspaper's lead story, which was that we are damaging our children by over protecting them; that they are not being allowed to play naturally. Another news story that day - where, tragically, a boy was killed on a motorway - shrieked, 'What were the parents doing allowing an 8-year old out alone?'

The decision-making dilemma parents face was clearly presented in the epiphany Maye had that day: do we protect our children too much, or not enough? Would we look after them better if we prioritised our own needs more than we sometimes do? As we keep trying to get the balance right in our families, the answers to these questions are not fixed. Our parenting, like life itself, is a living thing, an organism that is constantly growing and changing. Perhaps the trick is in keeping our attitudes fluid.

As you approach the strategies we have shared here, aiming to be fluid may help you adapt and shape them to keep the balance in your family.

We wish you the best with it.

dreams COME true

how rainbow the over somewhere

There are more examples and ideas on www.celebratingfamilies.co.uk

While Georgie dreams of working with animals or being a photographer, as parents our hopes for her future are much more specific. We dream of her having her own home and getting the support she needs to lead a full life and get a job. One simple dream we desire for Georgie's future is that it is filled with hope, healing and new beginnings and that she continues to accept people just the way they are

Reflections

Helen

I hope you may have seen that Celebrating Families has been a very personal work for us. It emerged as my team at Helen Sanderson Associates and I learned, through more than ten years of supporting people with learning disabilities, about person centred thinking and planning. Michael Smull and the Learning Community for Person Centred Practices developed most of these original tools. We quickly saw that the person centred thinking tools we were teaching were just as applicable in our own lives. We would begin our team meetings with stories about how we were using these tools with our families. When I shared what we had been doing with John O'Brien, one of the originators of person centred planning, he challenged me to put our stories in a book. We set ourselves the goal of creating such a book.

Maye

When Helen asked me if I would be interested in working with her to finish off this book, and I read what she had written, it resonated so much with my personal experiences. Many of her techniques, I saw, were systematic representations of what I had instinctively tried to do with my own children a generation before. What Helen had written also resonated with my professional life: as teacher, trainer, therapist and coach, I have spent around 40 years listening to people talk about their lives. When they spoke, what these women were experiencing in their families always took centre stage. I recognised the value of offering mothers practical help to enhance the quality of their family lives as much as possible – so of course I accepted Helen's offer to join the project.

Notes

Chapter 2: Sharing What We Know

P. 10   Helen Harcombe (2005) *Mother Nurture*. Article in the Daily Mail (pp. 35 and 38)
         May 2nd 2005

Chapter 3: Appreciating Each Other

P. 34   Stephen Biddulph (1998) *The Secret of Happy Children* (London: Thorsons) p. 5
P. 37   Nancy Kline (1999) *Time to Think: Listening to Ignite the Human Mind* (London:
         Ward Lock) p. 62
P. 39   Stephen Biddulph (1998) *The Secret of Happy Children* p. 12
P. 41   Nancy Kline (1999) *Time to Think: Listening to Ignite the Human Mind*
P. 43   Stephen Biddulph (1998) *The Secret of Happy Children* p. 17

Chapter 5: Communication In Your Family

P. 59   Stephen Biddulph (1998) *The Secret of Happy Children* (London: Thorsons) p. 52
P. 60   Nancy Kline (1999) *Time to Think: Listening to Ignite the Human Mind* (London:
         Ward Lock) p.44

Chapter 6: A Question Of Values

P. 69   Steven Covey (1998) *The 7 Habits of Highly Effective Families* (London: Simon and
         Shuster Ltd) p. 71-72
P. 70   Dalai Lama (2001) *Instructions For Life in the New Millennium* (Melbourne: Dynamo
         House) p. 2
P. 70   Steven Covey (1998) *The 7 Habits of Highly Effective Families*
P. 73   Steven Covey (1998) *The 7 Habits of Highly Effective Families*
P. 74   Steven Covey (1998) *The 7 Habits of Highly Effective Families*

Chapter 7: Belonging

P. 88   David Futrelle, *Can Money Buy Happiness?* Accessed 29/04/07
         http://money.cnn.com/magazines/moneymag/moneymag_
         archive/2006/08/01/8382225/index.htm

Chapter 9: Dreams, Hopes and Wishes

P. 113   Michael Fordyce, *Psychology of Happiness*. Accessed 29/04/07
          http://www.gethappy.net.bklt10.htm
P. 114   Victor Frankl (1985) *Man's Search for Meaning taken from What is Spiritual Freedom?* Accessed 29/04/07
          http://happinessblog.com/archives/category/happiness-quotes/
P. 115   J.K. Rowling, *Happiness Choices Show Who We Are*. Accessed 29/04/07
          http://happinessblog.com/archives/category/happiness-quotes/

For Further Information

www.celebratingfamilies.co.uk
www.helensandersonassociates.co.uk
www.learningcommunity.us

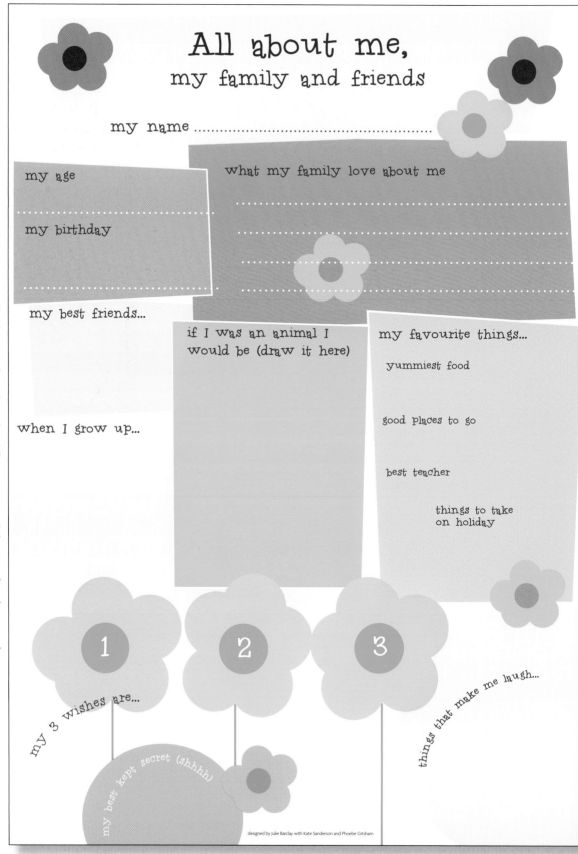

All about me,
my family and friends

my name ....

my age

my birthday

what my family love about me

my best friends...

when I grow up...

if I was an animal I would be (draw it here)

my favourite things...

yummiest food

good places to go

best teacher

things to take on holiday

1

2

3

my 3 wishes are...

my best kept secret (shhhh)

things that make me laugh...

designed by Julie Barclay with Kate Sanderson and Phoebe Gitsham

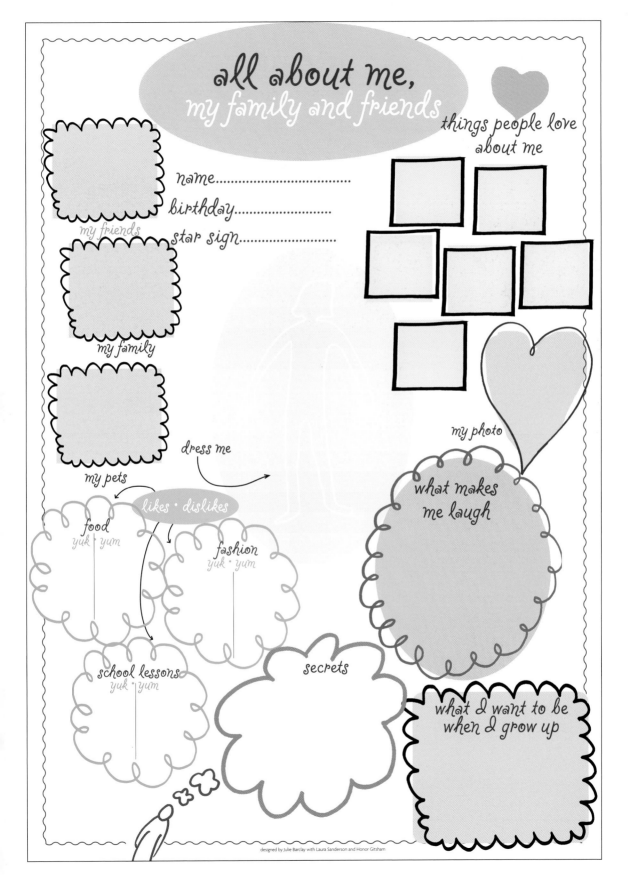

Acknowledgements

If it takes a village to raise a child, it takes a community to create a book.

Thank you to our community of family, friends, colleagues, and artists, who have made this book possible.

There are many voices of experience shared in the pages of this book, through words and illustrations. Thank you to all the people who contributed their stories and ideas:
Jo Harvey, Charlotte Sweeney, Michelle Livesley, Ruth Gorman, Louise Skelhorn, Lorraine Erwin, Gill Bailey, Julie Bray, Barbara Bailey, Julie Allen, Julie Lunt, Jonathan Ralphs, Deb Watson, Amanda George, Jayne Cooper, Rachel Scott, Carolyn Sanderson, Clare Sanderson and Miguel Pinedo, Suzie Franklin, Wendy and Dave Blundell, Harold Pryme, Nik and Julian Gitsham, Neil and Alison Woodhead, Lynn James-Jenkinson, Gill Goodwin, Sarah and Adam Craggs, Jo Kennedy, James and Angela Mountstephens, Ian and Anna Waugh.

Thank you to the people who created the examples and scrap book pages. They are Ruth Mathiesen, Gill Cosford, Mandy Anderson, Julie Barclay, Wendy Blundell, Nicola Becci at Soremi Jewellery, Sue Leckonby, Laura Winderbank, Rig Out, Lyn Antley. These were photographed by Anne Bennison.

In going from ideas to draft, redraft and to this final version, we are indebted to Robert Graham, for his editing skills, David Cohen, Jo Selley for her proofreading and Barbara Bailey for her support.

The impact of this book is a synthesis of words and design. The book has been designed by Julie Barclay, the third 'author' in our eyes.

The wealth of materials on person centred thinking and planning comes from the Learning Community for Person Centred Practices, and from the pioneers of person centred planning with people with learning disabilities. We would particularly like to acknowledge the contributions of Michael Smull and John O'Brien, who gave us the original idea for this book.

We are sharing proceeds from the book with the Learning Community for Person Centred Practices and with the HSA Foundation, a charity for social justice.

This is work in progress, and we are sharing more examples and ideas on the website www. celebratingfamilies.co.uk. We would love to hear from you - your stories and examples.

Finally, we would like to thank and appreciate our own families, for all their support in making this book possible, and for sharing their experiences. Thank you to Katherine, Robert, Andy, Ellie, Laura and Kate.

Helen Sanderson
Maye Taylor
January 2008

Appendix

These are the person centred thinking tools that appear in the book.

Person centred thinking tool	What it does	Examples in this book
Sorting Important To/For	Sorts what is important to someone (what makes us happy, content, fulfilled) from what is important for them (to keep them healthy and safe). Provides information to help obtain a balance between the two.	Chapter 2 explains how you can describe and learn more about what is important to your child. We introduce one-page profiles, which describe the balance between what is important to the child, and the support that they need (important for them). The example one page profiles are: Laura, Cameron, Josh and Flo. This approach is also used with families, and Lou, John and Jos' family plan is an example.
The Doughnut Sort	This identifies specific responsibilities - core responsibilities, where you can use creativity and judgement, and what you are not responsible for.	In Chapter 5 you can see the doughnut that Fiona and Tim developed.

Person centred thinking tool	What it does	Examples in this book
Matching	This is a structure to look at both what skills / supports and what people characteristics make for good matches.	In Chapter 2 the matching tool is used to find a nanny or childminder for Shannon.
Communication chart	This tool helps to focus on communication, particularly when children don't use many words.	In Chapter 5 you can see Josh and Jos' communication chart.
Sorting Working/Not Working	Clarifies what to build on and what to change.	Karen and Andrew used Working/Not working with the family in Chapter 5.
Decision Making Agreement	This tool clarifies who makes what decisions in a particular situation.	You can read Evie's decision making agreement in Chapter 5.
Like And Admire	This is a simple way of recording someone's gifts and characteristics.	You can see Rosie's like and admire poster in Chapter 3.

For more examples and ideas, go to
www.celebratingfamilies.co.uk

For information about person centred thinking tools, and person centred planning go to
www.helensandersonassociates.co.uk and
www.learningcommunity.us